Microsoft® **MAIL** For Windows™

Version 3.0b or later

Step by Step

and Microsoft Schedule +

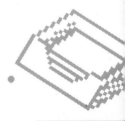

Catapult

MicrosoftPress

PUBLISHED BY
Microsoft Press
A Division of Microsoft Corporation
One Microsoft Way
Redmond, Washington 98052-6399

Library of Congress Cataloging-in-Publication Data pending.

   ISBN 1-55615-571-9

Printed and bound in the United States of America.

1 2 3 4 5 6 7 8 9 MLML 8 7 6 5 4 3

Distributed to the book trade in Canada by Macmillan of Canada, a division of Canada Publishing Corporation.

Distributed to the book trade outside the United States and Canada by Penguin Books Ltd.

Penguin Books Ltd., Harmondsworth, Middlesex, England
Penguin Books Australia Ltd., Ringwood, Victoria, Australia
Penguin Books N.Z. Ltd., 182-190 Wairau Road, Auckland 10, New Zealand

British Cataloging-in-Publication Data pending.

AT&T and Easylink are registered trademarks of American Telephone and Telegraph Company. AppleTalk is a registered trademark of Apple Computer, Inc. Banyan is a registered trademark of Banyan Systems, Inc. cc:Mail is a trademark of cc:Mail, Inc., a wholly owned subsidiary of Lotus Development Corporation. CompuServe is a registered trademark of CompuServe, Inc. Infonet is a registered trademark of Computer Sciences Corporation. Data General is a registered trademark of Data General Corporation. All-In-1, DEC, and VMS are registered trademarks of Digital Equipment Corporation. AS/400, IBM, OfficeVision, and PROFS are registered trademarks of International Business Corporation. Lotus Notes is a registered trademark of Lotus Development Corporation. Microsoft, MS, and MS-DOS are registered trademarks and Windows and the Windows operating system logo are trademarks of Microsoft Corporation. Cooperation is a registered trademark of NCR. Novell is a registered trademark of Novell, Inc. Retix is a registered trademark of Retix. Unisys is a registered trademark of Unisys Corporation. Unix is a registered trademark of UNIX Systems Laboratories. WANG is a registered trademark of Wang Laboratories.

For Catapult, Inc.
Managing Editor: Donald Elman
Author: Samantha J.W. Robertson

For Microsoft Press
Acquisitions Editor: Marjorie Schlaikjer
Project Editor: Casey D. Doyle

WE'VE CHOSEN THIS SPECIAL LAY-FLAT BINDING
to make it easier for you to work through the step-by-step lessons while you're at your computer.

With little effort, you can make this book lie flat when you open it to any page. Simply press down on the inside (where the paper meets the binding) of any left-hand page, and the book will stay open to that page. You can open the book this way every time. The lay-flat binding will not weaken or crack over time.

It's tough, flexible, sturdy—and designed to last.

Contents

Part 1   Microsoft Mail for Windows Basics

Part 2   Working with Microsoft Mail for Windows

About This Book

Microsoft Mail for Windows helps you improve your communication with your colleagues. Microsoft Schedule+ works hand in hand with Microsoft Mail for Windows to help you get and maintain control of your schedule and coordinate with other people's schedules. *Microsoft Mail for Windows Step by Step* shows you how to use Microsoft Mail for Windows and Microsoft Schedule+ to simplify your work and increase your productivity. You can use *Microsoft Mail for Windows Step by Step* in a classroom setting, or you can use it as a tutorial to learn Microsoft Mail for Windows and Microsoft Schedule+ at your own pace and at your own convenience.

You also get hands-on practice using the files on the accompanying disk. Instructions for copying the practice files to your computer's hard disk are in "Getting Ready," the next section in this book.

Working with Different Versions of Microsoft Mail

This book is designed to be compatible with Microsoft Mail for Windows versions 3.0b and 3.2. Some features of other versions, such as 3.0 and 3.1 (the Windows for Workgroups version), are slightly different. Version 3.0 does not include the ability to import or export files, which is required to complete several lessons in this book. Version 3.1 does not have a spelling checker, online demonstrations, or a Help Index. Significant differences between the versions are noted in the text where appropriate.

Finding the Best Starting Point for You

This book is designed for new users learning Microsoft Mail for Windows and Microsoft Schedule+ for the first time, and for experienced users who want to learn and use the new features in Microsoft Mail for Windows. Even if you are a novice user, *Microsoft Mail for Windows Step by Step* will help you get the most out of Microsoft Mail for Windows and Microsoft Schedule+.

This book is divided into three major parts, each containing several related lessons. At the end of each part, you will find a Review & Practice section that gives you the opportunity to practice the skills you learned in that part. Each Review & Practice section allows you to test your knowledge and prepare for your own work.

Use the following table to determine your best path through the book.

If you are	Follow these steps
New to a computer or graphical environment, such as Microsoft Windows	Read "Getting Ready," the next section in this book, and follow the instructions to install the practice files. Carefully read the sections on "If You Are New to Microsoft Windows" and "If You Are New To Using a Mouse." Next, work through Lessons 1 and 2 for a basic introduction to Microsoft Mail for Windows. Work through Lessons 3, 4, 5, and 6 in any order. Then, if you have Microsoft Schedule+, work through Lessons 7, 8, and 9.
Familiar with the Microsoft Windows graphical computer environment, but new to using electronic mail or Microsoft Mail for Windows	Follow the instructions for installing the practice files in the "Getting Ready" section in this book. Next, work through Lessons 1 and 2. Work through Lessons 3, 4, 5, and 6 in any order. Then, if you have Microsoft Schedule+ installed, work through Lessons 7, 8, and 9.
Familiar with Microsoft Windows and Microsoft Mail, but new to using scheduling programs or Microsoft Schedule+	Follow the instructions for installing the practice files in the "Getting Ready" section in this book. Next, review any parts of Lessons 1 through 6 that cover topics about Microsoft Mail with which you have little experience. Then, work through Lessons 7, 8, and 9.

Using This Book As a Classroom Aid

If you're an instructor, you can use *Microsoft Mail for Windows Step by Step* for teaching computer users. You may want to select certain lessons that meet your students' needs and incorporate your own demonstrations into the lessons.

If you plan to teach the entire contents of this book, you should probably set aside at least a full day of classroom time to allow for discussion, questions, and any customized practice you may create. Lessons 1 and 2 cover Microsoft Mail for Windows basics like sending and receiving mail. Lessons 3 through 6 cover attaching files, embedding objects, organizing messages, setting Microsoft Mail for Windows options, and working offline. Lessons 7 through 9 cover the basics of Microsoft Schedule+ including working with the Appointment Book, the Task list, the Planner, and the Messages Window.

Conventions Used in This Book

Before you start any of the lessons, it's important that you understand the terms and notational conventions used in this book.

Procedural Conventions

- Hands-on exercises that you are to follow are given in numbered lists of steps (1, 2, and so on). A triangular bullet (▶) indicates an exercise with only one step.

- The word *choose* is used for carrying out a command from a menu or a dialog box.

- The word *select* is used for highlighting directories, filenames, text boxes, and menu bars and options, and for selecting options in a dialog box.

Notational Conventions

- Characters or commands that you type appear in **bold lowercase** type.

- Important terms (where first defined) and titles of books appear in *italic* type.

- Names of files, paths, or directories appear in ALL CAPITALS, except when they are to be directly typed in.

Keyboard Conventions

- Names of keys that you press are in small capital letters, for example, TAB and SHIFT.

- A plus sign (+) between two key names means that you must press those keys at the same time. For example, "Press ALT+TAB" means that you hold down the ALT key while you press TAB.

- A comma (,) between two or more key names means that you must press each of the keys consecutively, not together. For example, "Press ALT, T, X" means that you press and release each key in sequence. "Press ALT+W, L" means that you first press ALT and W together, and then release them and press L.

- You can choose menu commands with the keyboard. Press the ALT key to activate the menu bar, and then sequentially press the keys that correspond to the highlighted or underlined letter of the menu name and of the command name. For some commands, you can also press a key combination listed in the menu.

- You can select or clear option buttons or check boxes in dialog boxes with the keyboard. Press the ALT key and then press the key that corresponds to the underlined letter of the option name. Or, you can press TAB until the option is highlighted, and then press the SPACEBAR to select or clear the option button or check box.

Mouse Conventions

- *Click* means to point to an object and then press and release the mouse button. For example, "Click the Compose tool." The word "click" is used for selecting command buttons, option buttons, and check boxes.

- *Drag* means to click and hold the mouse button while you move the mouse. For example, "Drag the Budgets message to the Miscellaneous folder."

- *Double-click* means to rapidly press and release the mouse button twice. For example, "Double-click the Microsoft Mail for Windows icon to start Microsoft Mail for Windows."

Other Features of This Book

- Text in the left margin provides tips, additional useful information, or keyboard alternatives.

- The "One Step Further" exercise at the end of each lesson introduces new options or techniques that build on the commands and skills you used in the lesson.

- Each lesson has a summary list of the skills you have learned in each lesson and gives a brief review of how to accomplish particular tasks.

- The optional "Review & Practice" activity at the end of each major part provides an opportunity to use all of the skills presented in the lessons of that part. These activities present problems that reinforce what you have learned and encourage you to recognize new ways that you can use Microsoft Mail for Windows and Microsoft Schedule+.

Cross-References to Microsoft Mail and Microsoft Schedule+ Documentation

References to the *Microsoft Mail for Windows User's Guide,* the *Microsoft Schedule+ User's Guide,* and online Help topics or demonstrations at the end of each lesson direct you to specific chapters or subjects for additional information. Notes and other references will also direct you to your Microsoft Mail for Windows or Microsoft Schedule+ documentation. Use these materials to take full advantage of the features in Microsoft Mail for Windows and Microsoft Schedule+.

Online Help

The Help system in both Microsoft Mail for Windows and Microsoft Schedule+ provides a complete online reference to Microsoft Mail for Windows and Microsoft Schedule+ operations. You learn more about the Help system in the Getting Ready section.

Microsoft Mail User's Guide and *Microsoft Schedule+ User's Guide*

These manuals include information about setting up and starting Microsoft Mail for Windows and Microsoft Schedule+, using the Help systems, working with the applications, and explanations of the applications' features.

Getting Ready

This section of the book prepares you for your first steps into the Microsoft Mail and Microsoft Schedule+ environments. You will review some useful Microsoft Windows techniques as well as terms and concepts important in your understanding of how to use Microsoft Mail and Microsoft Schedule+.

You will learn:

- How to install the step-by-step practice files on your computer's hard disk.

- How to start Microsoft Windows.

- How to start Microsoft Mail and Microsoft Schedule+.

- About important features of the windows, menus, and dialog boxes in the Microsoft Windows graphical environment.

- How to use the online Help system in Microsoft Mail and Microsoft Schedule+.

What Is Electronic Mail?

Electronic mail is your computer's version of the postal service or interoffice mail. Instead of hand delivering paper documents, you send them through the network to other computer users. With electronic mail, you can send messages to and receive messages from other people who are either on, or have access to, your computer network. Electronic messages are stored either in your own electronic mailbox or on the server, from which you can forward or reply to them as you please.

With Microsoft Mail, you can send courtesy copies of messages to other people. You can also attach electronic documents or other files to send along with your messages. You can organize your messages into folders or sort them, and you can even print them if you need a paper copy. Microsoft Mail informs you whenever you receive a new message.

Installing the Step by Step Practice Files

Included with this book is a disk called "Practice Files for Microsoft Mail for Windows Step by Step." These files are copied to your hard disk into a special PRACTICE directory created in the MSMAIL directory in which Microsoft Mail is stored on your computer. A special program on the Practice Files disk automatically installs these files for you.

Copy the practice files to your hard disk

1   Turn on your computer.

2   Insert the Practice Files disk into drive A or B of your computer.

3   If you have Windows running, open the Program Manager and choose <u>R</u>un from the <u>F</u>ile menu. If not, skip to step 5.

4   In the File name box, type **a:\install** and choose OK.

5   At the MS-DOS command prompt (usually "C:\>"), type **a:\install** (or **b:\install**).

Be sure to type a backslash (\) between the colon (:) and "install."

6   Follow the instructions on the screen.

The installation process copies the files from your practice disk and places them on your hard disk. Since you still have a copy available on the practice disk when this process is complete, you can reuse the original files later if you want to repeat a lesson or try a new option.

Lesson Background

The practice files are used in certain lessons to simulate what you might encounter using Microsoft Mail or Microsoft Schedule+ in a typical business setting. For these lessons, imagine that you work in the marketing department of West Coast Sales. West Coast Sales wants to update its image with a new company logo, and has put the marketing group in charge of the project. As an important member of the marketing group, you are also involved in creating the department budget and trying to plan the department's strategy for the next quarter. Throughout these lessons, you use Microsoft Mail and Microsoft Schedule+ to assist you in communicating with others in marketing, as well as throughout West Coast Sales, and in scheduling times for your planning sessions. For some of the exercises, such as reading incoming mail, you play the role of "Kris Mueller." For other exercises, such as sending messages over your real network, you will use your own name.

Starting Microsoft Windows, Mail, and Schedule+

The first and second parts of this book assume that you have Microsoft Windows and Mail installed on your system, and that you are connected to a network. The third part also requires that you have Microsoft Schedule+ running. After you install Microsoft Mail and Microsoft Schedule+ and install the practice files, you can start Microsoft Windows, Mail, and Schedule+.

Use the following procedures to start Windows and Microsoft Mail. Your screen might be different from the following illustrations, depending on your particular setup and the applications installed on your computer. For more information about Windows, see the *Microsoft Windows User's Guide*.

Start Windows from the MS-DOS command prompt

1 At the command prompt, type **win**

2 Press ENTER.

After the initial startup, the Program Manager window looks like the following illustration. You can start all of your applications, including Microsoft Mail and Microsoft Schedule+, from Program Manager.

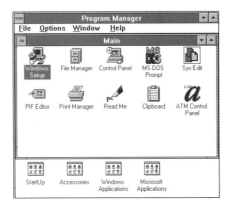

When Microsoft Windows is active, everything on your screen (called the *desktop*) is displayed in *windows*. You can adjust each window to the size you want and you can move windows anywhere you want on the desktop. You can have multiple windows open at the same time to compare and share information easily.

The Program Manager window   Within the Program Manager window are symbols that represent applications and documents. These symbols, called *icons,* are used to open the applications they represent. The icons are organized in groups, usually related to applications. The default installation of Microsoft Mail and Microsoft Schedule+ creates a group named Microsoft Applications and an icon within that group for each application.

As you become more familiar with Windows, you will find that you can customize the startup screen to your personal working style.

The Microsoft Applications group   Double-clicking the Microsoft Applications group icon opens the Microsoft Applications program group window that holds the icons for Microsoft Mail and Microsoft Schedule+. Before you can use Microsoft Mail, you must know the mailbox name and password that your system administrator has assigned to you.

Start Microsoft Mail

1 Double-click the Microsoft Applications group icon.

This opens the Microsoft Applications program group.

2 Double-click the Microsoft Mail program icon.

Microsoft Mail

Some installations might not require you to type your name or password. Skip step 3 or 4 if your installation does not require you to type your name or password.

3 Type your mailbox name, and then press TAB.

4 Type your password, and then press ENTER.

5 If you do not have Microsoft Schedule+, click the Maximize button on the Microsoft Mail application window and skip the next exercise.

Start Microsoft Schedule+

If you have Microsoft Schedule+ on your system, you can start it now.

1 Double-click the Microsoft Schedule+ program icon.

Microsoft
Schedule+

Note   Microsoft Schedule+ uses the same name and password as Microsoft Mail. If you have already started Microsoft Mail, you will not need to retype these words. If you start Microsoft Schedule+ before having started Microsoft Mail, you will need to type your mailbox name and then your password. If you later change your password in Microsoft Mail, you will need to use the new one in Microsoft Schedule+ as well.

---

2 Click the Minimize button in the Microsoft Schedule+ window.

This leaves Microsoft Schedule+ running, but minimized at the bottom of the screen.

3 Click the Maximize button in the Microsoft Mail window.

If You Are New to Microsoft Windows

For new Microsoft Windows users, this section provides a general overview of what you can accomplish within this graphical environment. Windows is designed to be easy to use while still allowing sophisticated functions. It helps you handle virtually all of the daily work that you carry out with your computer. Microsoft Windows provides a common interface among many different application programs—both in the way they share data and in the way you control their operations.

After you become familiar with the basic elements of Microsoft Windows, you can apply these skills to learn and use Microsoft Mail and Microsoft Schedule+, as well as many other types of applications including word processing, graphics, or spreadsheets.

Using Microsoft Windows

The following illustration shows some of the common elements that are found in the Microsoft Mail for Windows interface and other Window-based applications.

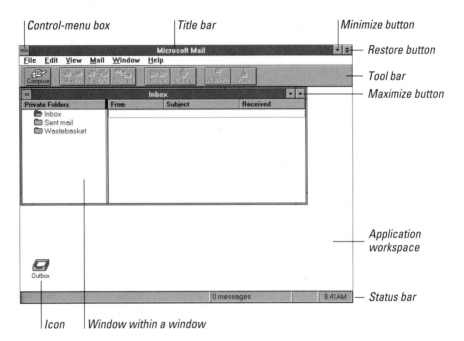

You can scroll, move, size, and close a window by using the mouse.

To	Do this
Scroll through a window	Click the scroll bars or drag the scroll box.
Change the size of a window	Drag any of the window edges or corners.
Enlarge a window to fill the screen	Double-click the title bar or click the Maximize button.
Shrink a window to an icon	Click the Minimize button.

To	Do this
Restore a window to its previous size	Click the Restore button.
Move a window	Drag the title bar.
Close a window	Double-click the Control-menu box.

Using Windows in Microsoft Mail

Like any Windows-based application, Microsoft Mail has a main program window that displays the application name, "Microsoft Mail," in the title bar. This window can be maximized to fill the entire screen, restored to fill part of the screen, or minimized to an icon at the bottom of the screen.

Within the application workspace, Mail can display at least two active windows. One of these represents the *Outbox*, which is a temporary holding area for messages that are sent to other people. Another, more important window shows lists of messages that are stored in different groups called *folders*, which are explained in Lesson 2. Each of these windows can be maximized, restored, or minimized within the application workspace of the Microsoft Mail window.

You can open additional windows in the workspace to show folder lists and the contents of individual messages. Any of these additional windows can be maximized, restored, or minimized within the application workspace. Except for the Outbox and one folder window, any additional windows can also be closed or removed from the workspace.

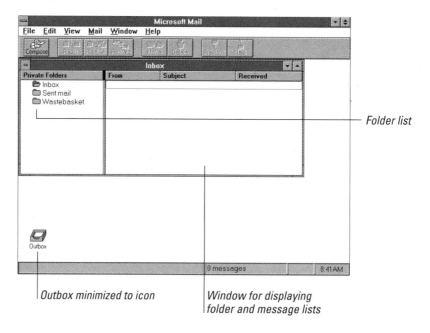

Folder list

Outbox minimized to icon

Window for displaying folder and message lists

Using Menus and Commands

In Microsoft Mail for Windows, menu names appear in the *menu bar* near the top of the screen. A list of commands appears when you click a menu. To choose a command, you click the menu name to open the menu and then click the command.

The following illustration shows the Microsoft Mail menu bar with the Edit menu displayed.

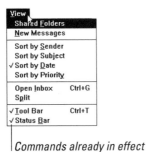

Shortcut keys

Some options have a *shortcut key* combination listed to the right of the command name. Once you are familiar with the menus and commands, these shortcut keys can save you time.

All commands have keyboard equivalents. If you are not using a mouse, you make selections by pressing ALT and the underlined character of the menu. To select a command from a menu, you can simply type the underlined character when the menu is displayed. See Appendix A for a list of keyboard equivalents and shortcuts.

When a command name appears dimmed, it doesn't apply to your current situation or is unavailable. For example, the Paste command on the Edit menu appears dimmed if you have not first used either the Copy or Cut command.

When a command name displays a check mark to its left, the command is already in effect.

The commands that are available on this menu might vary depending on which window is active.

Commands already in effect

To close a menu without choosing a command, click the menu again.

When you need to supply information for a command to proceed, a *dialog box* appears on the screen. After you enter information or make selections in the dialog box, you can click the OK button with the mouse or press the ENTER key to carry out the command. You can also choose the Cancel button or press ESC to close a dialog box without carrying out an action.

Using Dialog Boxes

When you choose a command that is followed by an ellipsis (. . .), Windows-based applications display a dialog box so that you can provide more information. Depending on the dialog box, you type the information or select from a group of options.

For example, the Print Setup dialog box is displayed when you choose the Print Setup command from the File menu. In the dialog box, you specify the options you want. The Print Setup dialog box looks like the following illustration.

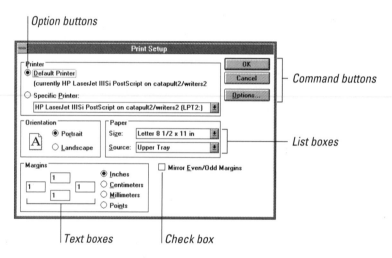

This dialog box appears in Schedule+.

Every dialog box has at least one or more of the following areas (called *controls*) to help you supply the information necessary to carry out the command.

Text box   You type information in a text box. For example, in the Options dialog box, you can type a file name to create an encapsulated PostScript file.

List box   Available choices appear in a list. If the list is longer than the box, you can use the scroll bar to see the rest of the list.

Option button   You can select only one option at a time from a group of option buttons. A selected option button has a black dot in its center.

Check box   You can select or clear the option in each check box independently from other check boxes. A selected check box has an X in its center.

Command button   You choose a command button to carry out an operation or to display more options. If a command button is dimmed, it is unavailable. An ellipsis following the name of a command button means that more options are available.

Choose the OK button to carry out an operation, choose Networks to open another dialog box with more options, or choose the Cancel button to cancel.

Selecting Dialog Box Options

To move around in a dialog box with the mouse, you can simply point to and click the item you want. From the keyboard you can hold down ALT and press the key for the underlined letter at the same time. Or you can press TAB to move between items and press SPACEBAR or the arrow keys to select and clear options.

Use the procedures in this table to select options in a dialog box with the mouse.

To	Do this
Select an option button	Click the option button.
Clear an option button	Select another option button.
Select or clear a check box	Click the check box.
Select an item in a list	Click the item.
Move to a text box	Click the text box.
Select text in a text box	Double-click a word or drag through the characters.
Select all text in a text box	Press CTRL+A.
Scroll through a list	Use the scroll bars.

Using the Tool Bar

Located below the menu bar is the *tool bar*. It contains buttons that are shortcuts for choosing some of the most commonly used commands in Microsoft Mail. For example, clicking the Compose button on the tool bar is the same as choosing the Compose Note command from the Mail menu.

Although initially you might feel more comfortable using the keyboard for making menu selections, it is generally faster to use the mouse to click a button on the tool bar. The instructions in this book emphasize using the tool bar as the most efficient method for the nearly all of the basic Microsoft Mail operations.

If You Are New to Using a Mouse

Menu bars, tool bars, and many other features of Microsoft Mail and other Windows-based applications were designed for working with a mouse. Although you can use the keyboard for most actions in Microsoft Mail, many of these actions are easier to do with the mouse.

Mouse Pointers

The mouse controls a symbol on the screen called the *pointer*. You move the pointer by sliding the mouse over a flat surface in the direction you want the pointer to move. If you run out of room to move the mouse, you can lift it up and put it down again. The pointer moves only when the mouse is touching a flat surface.

Moving the mouse pointer across the screen does not affect the document; the pointer simply indicates a location on the screen. When you press the mouse button, an action occurs at the location of the pointer.

When the mouse pointer passes over different parts of the Microsoft Mail window, it changes shape, indicating what you can do with it at that point. Most of your work in this book will use the following mouse pointers.

This pointer	Appears when you point to
$\uparrow\!\!\!\searrow$	The menu bar and tool bars to choose a command, a button, the title bar, and the scroll bars.
I	Text in a text box. When you click the mouse in a text box, the pointer is called the insertion point.
ᕗ	A topic in Help.

Using the Mouse

These are the four basic mouse actions that you use throughout the lessons in this book.

Pointing   Moving the mouse to place the pointer on an item is called *pointing*.

Clicking   Pointing to an item on your screen and then quickly pressing and releasing the mouse button once is called *clicking*. You select items on the screen and move around in a document by clicking.

Double-clicking   Pointing to an item and then quickly pressing and releasing the primary mouse button (usually the left mouse button) twice is called *double-clicking*. This is a convenient shortcut for many tasks in Microsoft Mail.

Dragging   Holding down the mouse button as you move the pointer is called *dragging*. You can use this technique to select data in the rows and columns in tables.

Try the mouse

Take a moment to test drive the mouse. Simply slide the mouse so that the pointer moves around the Microsoft Mail screen.

1 Slide the mouse until the pointer is over the menus and tools at the top of the screen. The pointer is now a left-pointing arrow.

2 Slide the mouse around the document window (the large open area in the center of the screen).

3 Click the Compose button and slide the mouse around the resulting Send Note form. The pointer now resembles an I-beam.

4 Double-click the Control-menu box on the Send Note form.

Warning   Because each window has a Control-menu box that you can double-click, be careful to note which window you are closing, especially when you want to close a window only and not leave Microsoft Mail or Microsoft Schedule+.

Using Help

Microsoft Mail and Microsoft Schedule+ both include a complete online Help reference system. You can access Help information in several ways.

To get Help information	Do this
By topics or activity	From the Help menu, choose Contents or Index.
While working in a window or dialog box	Press F1.

Note   Version 3.1 of Microsoft Mail (the Windows for Workgroups version) does not include the Help Index or context-sensitive Help (F1).

Display the list of Help topics

▶ From the Help menu, choose Contents.

The Microsoft Mail Help Contents window looks like the following illustration.

You can size, move, and scroll through a Help window. You can switch between the Help window and Microsoft Mail or Microsoft Schedule+, or you can arrange the Help and application windows side by side so you can refer to Help while you work.

Getting Help on Help

To learn how you can make best use of all the information in Help, you can choose the Instructions button in the Help Contents screen.

Learn to use Help

1   Click the Instructions button in the Contents screen.

The Quick Help instructions topic appears.

2   Click the Contents button at the top to return to the Contents screen.

Note   You could also choose the Back button to return to the Contents screen. Choosing the Back button in the Help window returns you to the previous Help topic, which is Contents in this example.

---

3   From the File menu, choose Exit.

Getting Help on a Specific Topic

The Help system allows you to find information on a topic in three ways. First, the Contents list allows you to choose from among a list of functionally organized topics and subtopics. Second, the Search option allows you to quickly locate help topics by using a key word. If you know the command or term you want help on, you can go directly to the topic. Third, the Index allows you to choose from an extensive list of terms and topics arranged alphabetically.

In the next exercises, you look for information in each of these three ways.

Use the Contents list

1   From the Help menu, choose Contents to display the Help window.

2   Click the phrase "Sending Messages."

A list of subtopics appears in a popup window.

3   Click the first topic in the list, Sending a Message.

The selected topic is displayed.

4   Locate the phrase "user name," which has a dotted underline, and click it.

A definition of the term appears in a popup box.

Note   Clicking an underlined term "jumps" you to a related topic. Clicking a term with a dotted underline displays a popup topic in a topic window. This window provides a definition or presents you with other topics to which you can jump.

---

5   Click anywhere on the Help window.

The definition popup box closes.

Search for a specific topic

1   Click the Search button.

2   In the Search dialog, type **finding**

This is the key word that will be searched for. The finding topic appears in the list.

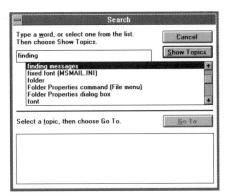

3   Choose the Show Topics button.

4   When the Finding a Message topic appears in the bottom of the Search dialog box, click the Go To button.

The Finding a message topic window appears.

Note   You will learn more about finding messages in Lesson 2. You can read this Help topic now to familiarize yourself with finding messages.

---

5   After you are done, double-click the Control-menu box in the upper-left corner of the Help window to close Help and return to the Microsoft Mail window.

Use the Help Index

Note   If you are using Microsoft Mail for Windows version 3.1 (the Windows for Workgroups version), skip this section. The Windows for Workgroups version does not include the Help index.

---

1   From the Help menu, choose Index.

The Help Index opens.

2   Click the Q button.

The Index jumps to the letter Q and lists all topics under that letter.

3   Click the topic "Quitting Mail."

Help opens and displays the related topic, "Signing In to or Out of Mail."

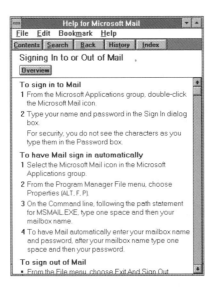

4   Double-click the Control-menu box on the Help window.

5   Double-click the Control-menu box on the Help Index window.

Quitting Microsoft Mail

You can also double-click the Control-menu box in the upper–left corner of the application window to leave Microsoft Mail.

▶   From the File menu, choose Exit .

You can also choose Exit and Sign Out to log off your network.

Note   Choosing Exit closes Microsoft Mail without logging you out of your mailbox. Choosing Exit and Sign Out closes Microsoft Mail and logs you out of your mailbox. If you are using Microsoft Mail-enabled programs, such as Microsoft Schedule+, Excel, or Word, you could use Exit to close Microsoft Mail and still be able to access your messages through these programs. Choosing Exit and Sign Out makes your mailbox inaccessible.

Quitting Microsoft Windows

If you would like to quit Windows, here is a simple way to exit the program.

Quit Microsoft Windows

1   Hold down the ALT key and press F4.

2   When you see a box with the message "This will end your Windows session," press ENTER.

Part 1

Microsoft Mail for Windows Basics

Composing and Sending Messages

When you need to inform others of an action or the status of a project, you can either walk over to their office and tell them or put a paper memo in their mail box down the hall. But a quicker, more efficient way to keep other people informed is to send them an electronic message through Microsoft Mail. When you use Microsoft Mail, you don't even need to leave your desk to send a memo or talk to someone.

When you want to send a note through Microsoft Mail, you begin by composing a new message. Microsoft Mail uses an electronic *form* to help you compose your message by entering information such as who you want the message to go to, what the message is about, and the text of the message. In this lesson, you will learn how to compose a new message, fill in the address information, enter and edit text, and send your message. You will also learn about such enhancements as address checking, groups, courtesy copies, and checking your spelling.

You will learn how to:

- Compose a message.
- Use the Address Book.
- Enter and edit message text.
- Send a message.

Estimated lesson time: 45 minutes

Start Microsoft Mail

1   In the Microsoft Applications group in the Program Manager, double-click the Microsoft Mail icon.

   For more information about starting Microsoft Mail, see "Starting Microsoft Mail" in the "Getting Ready" section earlier in this book.

2   Type your name and password, and then press ENTER.

   The Microsoft Mail window appears, ready for you to compose a new message.

3   Click the Maximize button on the Microsoft Mail application window, if is not already maximized.

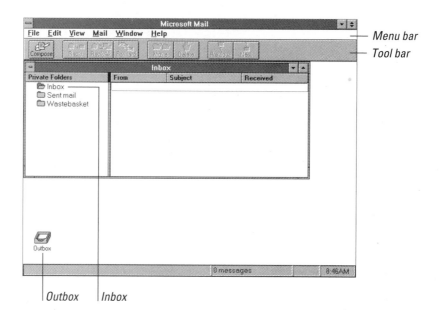

Composing a Simple Message

You can save a lot of time by using Microsoft Mail for all of your interoffice communications. A memo that could require five minutes of adjusting margins, getting the headings just right, and printing with a word processor might take only a few seconds to compose in Microsoft Mail. Because you send it through the network, there's no need to wait for a printer and, because Microsoft Mail has a standard form to fill in, there's no need to worry about setting up a page format.

When you compose a new message, you first open a form called the *Send Note* form, and then fill in information such as an address and text. These first steps are called *composing*. The Send Note form helps you fill in the information you need to send a message. Like many paper forms you've used before, the Send Note form has some areas that you must fill in, and other areas that are optional. The To text box, for example, is an area that you must fill in, while the Cc and Subject text boxes can be blank. Once the address and text are in place, you can send the message.

You can use either of two methods to compose a new message—click a button on the tool bar or choose a command from a menu. In the following exercise, you compose a simple message and send it to yourself.

Compose and send a new message

1   Locate the Compose button on the tool bar.

The Compose button is the far–left button on the tool bar, and looks like this:

2   Click the Compose button.

You can also choose Compose <u>N</u>ote from the <u>M</u>ail menu to accomplish the same thing. The Send Note form opens.

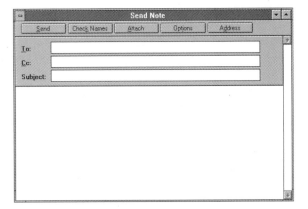

3   Click in the To text box to place your insertion point, and then type your name.

4   Click in the Subject box (or press TAB twice), and then type **Testing**

5   Move the insertion point to the text area and type **Testing the Mail system**.

Your message should look like this:

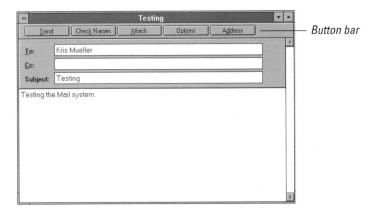

6   Click the Send button on the Send Note form, or press ALT+S.

Your message is sent.

When you receive the message you have sent to yourself, you might hear a beep or chime and the new message will appear in your Inbox. You'll learn about receiving and reading your incoming messages in Lesson 2.

On the simplest level, the steps you just carried out are all you have to do to compose and send a message with Microsoft Mail for Windows. The program, however, has many built-in features and options that can save you time or enhance your communications with other Mail users on the network. You will work with some of these features in the rest of this lesson.

Addressing Messages

You can address a message to one person, to several people, or to a group of people. To address a message to one person, you simply type the person's name in the To text box in the Send Note form. To add more people, you type a semicolon and a space, add the next name, and then repeat for each additional name. Don't worry about running out of space for names—the box will expand to fit as many names as you need.

Using Check Names

Microsoft Mail requires a complete name in order to send a message. You can always type the complete name in the To box, but Microsoft Mail includes a shortcut to save you time and typing. You can use the *Check Names button* in the Send Note box to find complete names from shortened versions that you type. You simply type the first few letters of a first or last name, click the Check Names button, and the name is filled in. The Check Names button can save you a lot of time if you have a long list of addresses or hard-to-spell names. It's also a quick way to find out if someone is not on your Mail network.

Use the Check Names button to address a message

1   Click the Compose button on the tool bar.

A Send Note form opens.

2   In the To box, type the first few letters of your name.

You might use the first part of either your first or last name to check.

3   Click the Check Names button, or press ALT+K.

Check Names looks at your list of possible addresses and locates your name. It fills in the To box with your complete name, which is underlined to show it is verified.

Note   If there is more than one name that begins with the letters you typed, a dialog box will open, asking you to choose the one you want. Select the name you want and choose OK.

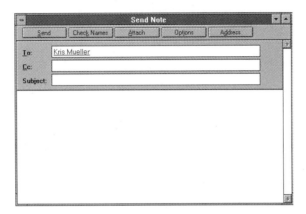

Sending Additional Copies of a Message

Suppose you are working on a project with several people. You need to send a message to one person in the group, directing that person to take some action, but you also need to keep the other people on the project informed. Rather than sending a message to one person and sending a separate message to all of the others, you can send one message with copies to everyone involved. You simply address the message to the person who needs to take action on it, and fill the other names in the *Courtesy copy*, or Cc, box.

Sending courtesy copies is a good way of keeping people, like a supervisor or a coworker, informed of the latest action being taken on a topic or project without sending a separate message directly to each of them. You can use the Check Names button to fill in names in the Cc box, just as you can use it in the To box.

Add a Courtesy Copy to your message

1   In the Cc box, type the name of a coworker who you know is connected to Mail.

2   Type a semicolon (;), a space, and then type another coworker's name who is on your Mail network.

3   Click the Check Names button.

   When you click Check Names, your full name is entered in the To box and your coworkers' full names are entered in the Cc box. Your message should look similar to the following illustration.

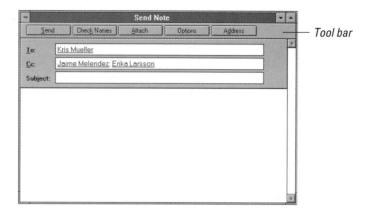

— Tool bar

Using the Address Book

Microsoft Mail for Windows provides an online *Address Book* that you can use to look up names. If you need to send a message to several people, you can scroll through the address book and select them all at once. Or, if you need to send a message to someone in another department but you are unsure of his or her name, you can look it up in the Address Book. You can address messages by typing a name and using the Check Names button, or you can also use the *Address button* on the Send Note tool bar. The Address button opens the Address Book, where you can select as many names as you need from the list of addresses.

You have access to two address books: the global Address Book that your network administrator sets up, and your *Personal Address Book*, which you can modify by adding or removing names. You will learn more about your Personal Address Book later in this lesson.

The Address Book that your administrator sets up is a master address list of all the people on your network or in your Mail system to whom you can send messages. You cannot add or delete names in this Address Book. You can, however, look up names in the Address Book when you are addressing a message.

Address a message with the Address Book

1   Select everything in the To text box, and then press DEL.

You will use the Address Book to place a name in the To text box.

2   Choose the Address button on the Send Note form, or press ALT+D.

The Address Book opens.

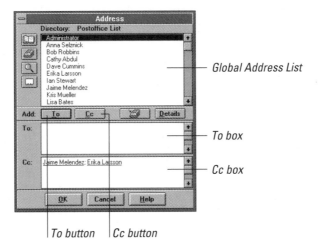

Global Address List

To box

Cc box

To button   Cc button

3 Scroll through the list at the top until you locate your name.

Tip Instead of scrolling through the list, you can type the first or first few letters of a name to go directly to that section of the Address Book.

4 Select your name, and then choose the To button, or press ALT+T.

Your name appears in the To box.

Note You can also double-click your name in the Address Book to place it in the To box.

5 Choose OK.

The Address Book closes and your name is filled in the To text box in the Send Note form.

Using Group Names

If you have a long list of people that you frequently send a message to, it can take a long time to enter their names even with the Check Names button or the Address Book. For sending messages to long lists of people, Microsoft Mail provides the *group name* feature. If you often send messages to the entire accounting staff, for example, you can set up an group that includes all of the people in that department and use a group name, such as "Accounting," instead of adding each individual name.

Your groups can include any people that you can send mail to through your postoffice. Your Microsoft Mail administrator might have already set up some groups for you to use. To use a group address that is already set up, you either type the group name in the To box or use the Address Book to specify the group name.

Address a message to an existing group

1   Select all of the text in the To box of your Send Note form, and then press DEL.

This deletes the address you typed earlier; you'll use a group name instead.

2   Click the Address button, or press ALT+D.

The Address dialog box opens and displays the Address Book.

Group name, in bold

3   Scroll through your Address Book until you find a group name.

Group names appear in bold in your Address Book.

Note   If you do not find a group name in the Address Book, leave the To text box blank and skip ahead to the next exercise—you will create a personal group then and can then use that group name.

---

4   Double-click a group name.

This selects the group from the list and places it in the To box.

5   Choose OK.

The Address dialog box closes and the group name is placed in the To box of your Send Note form.

Creating Personal Groups

Suppose you're working on a project and you often send messages to the other people on the same project. Your administrator might have created some groups that you can use, but you might not find a group with the particular members that you need. You could type all of their names each time you send a message, or you can set up your own personal group. You can create your own groups with the Personal Groups command on the Mail menu. Personal groups appear only in your Personal Address Book. To create a personal group, you simply choose the Personal Groups command, pick a name, and add the members of the group.

Create a personal group

1 From the Mail menu, choose Personal Groups.

The Personal Groups dialog box opens.

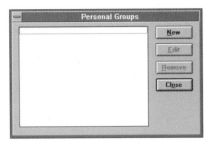

2 Click the New button.

The New Group dialog box opens.

3 Type **SBS Staff** and then click Create, or press ENTER.

Your new group called SBS Staff is created and the Address Book opens so you can select members to include in the group.

4 Click the first name in the list.

5 Click the Add button.

6 Click another name in the list.

7 Click the Add button.

Note If you want to select a longer series of names, press SHIFT or CTRL as you click the mouse. SHIFT selects every item in a list consecutively between the first and last item you select. To select multiple names that are not consecutive, use CTRL. While holding down CTRL, click each name that you want.

---

8 Click OK.

The Address Book closes and the Personal Groups dialog box reappears. The names are added to your new group, SBS Staff, in your Personal Group list.

Modify a personal group

Because you will be sending messages to this group, and you do not want to disturb other people in your office with your practice messages in this exercise, you will modify the group to include only yourself.

1 In the Personal Groups dialog box, check to be sure that SBS Staff is selected, and then choose Edit.

2 Select all names in the Group Members box, and then press DEL.

3 Scroll through the Address list and select your name, and then choose the Add button.

4 Choose OK.

5 Click the Close button.

SBS Staff is changed to include only your name, and the Personal Groups dialog box closes.

Address a message to a personal group

1 Select all of the text in the To box of your Send Note form, and then press DEL.

This deletes the group address you typed earlier; you'll use your new personal group instead.

2 Click the Address button or press ALT+D.

The Address dialog box opens and displays the Address Book.

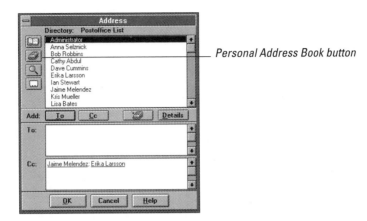

Personal Address Book button

3   Click the Personal Address Book button, which looks like a card file.

Your Personal Address Book opens with your new group, SBS Staff, included.

4   Double-click the group SBS Staff.

This selects the group from the list and places it in the To box.

5   Choose OK.

The Address dialog box closes and the group name is placed in the To box of your Send Note form.

Entering and Editing Text

Entering text in a message is like typing a memo with a word processor. You simply place your insertion point in the text area and start typing. Now that you have completed addressing your message, you are ready to enter the text.

Enter text in a new message

1   Press TAB twice to move to the Subject box.

If you include a subject for each message, it will be easier to locate the messages later. Try to make your subject headers as precise as possible so that stored messages are easier to identify.

2   Type **Planning Meeting** and then press TAB.

Pressing TAB moves you to the text area of the Send Note form.

3   Type **The monthly planning meeting will be held next Friday at 10:00 in the conference room.**

Your message should look like the following illustration.

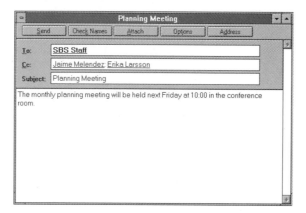

Editing the Contents of a Message

You will often need to add something to a message, reword a section, or correct typographical errors before sending a message. You can do most of the editing you need with the Cut, Copy, and Paste commands from the Edit menu. The Cut command removes the selected information and places it on the Clipboard for later use. The Copy command copies the selected information and places it on the Clipboard. The Paste command takes whatever is on the Clipboard and places it in your message, wherever your insertion point is. You can insert new text wherever you need to or you can delete sections. In the next exercise, you change the Cc address, add a sentence at the beginning of your message, delete a word, and then move the new sentence to the end of the message.

Edit a message

1   Select the names in the Cc box and press DEL.

2   Click in the text area, in front of the existing text.

   The insertion point should be right before the word "The".

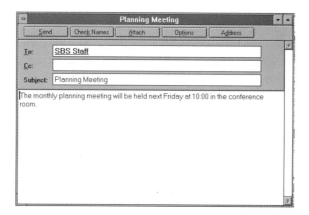

3 Type **Mark your calendars!** and press SPACEBAR.

The new sentence is added before your earlier text.

4 Locate the word "held" and double-click it.

Double-clicking is a quick way to select, or highlight, a whole word.

5 Press DEL.

The word "held" is deleted from the sentence.

6 Drag to select "Mark your calendars!" and the blank space following it.

7 From the Edit menu, choose Cut.

You will move this to the end of the message instead.

Note   When you cut, copy, and paste information, it is stored in a special part of memory called the Clipboard. When you paste the information, it is copied back from the Clipboard. You can paste a particular piece of information as many times as you need to, as long as you do not copy or cut anything else. When you copy or cut something else, the information stored in the Clipboard is erased and the new information replaces the old information. The information stored in the Clipboard is also erased whenever you quit Windows.

---

8 Click at the end of the message, and press SPACEBAR.

9 From the Edit menu, choose Paste.

The sentence is pasted at the end of the message. Your message looks similar to the following.

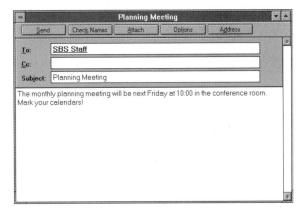

Checking the Spelling of a Message

Note   If you are working with Microsoft Mail for Windows version 3.1 (the Windows for Workgroups version), skip this section. The Windows for Workgroups version of Microsoft Mail does not include the spelling checker.

When you are working with important messages, you need to present the information you are sending clearly and accurately. To help you with accuracy, Microsoft Mail includes a *spelling checker*. The spelling checker used in Microsoft Mail will check the spelling in your document and look for misspelled or duplicated words. Microsoft Mail comes with a spelling checker similar to that included with Microsoft Word for Windows and Microsoft Excel.

To use the spelling checker, you choose Spelling from the Edit menu, and the spelling checker will begin to look through your document. If the spelling checker finds a misspelled word, it will show you the word in the Spelling dialog box and let you choose whether to ignore it, change it, or add it to the *dictionary*. The dictionary is the list of words that the spelling checker uses when checking your spelling. You can add words to the dictionary, such as names of people or products that you use often in your messages, so that the spelling checker will recognize them.

If the spelling checker finds a duplicated word (a word typed twice in a row), it will ask whether you want to delete the second occurrence of the word or ignore it. If the spelling checker is able to go through the entire message without finding any problems with your spelling, it will display a dialog box telling you that no misspelled words were found.

Check your message's spelling

1   Click at the beginning of your message text and type **Tsting spelling spelling**, and then press SPACEBAR.

Note   Because this is a practice session, you need to add something for the spelling checker to find in this exercise. Be sure you misspell the word "Testing" as "Tsting".

2   From the Edit menu, choose Spelling, or press F7.

The Spelling dialog box opens.

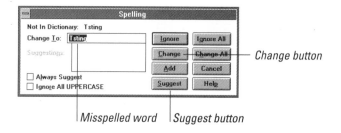

3   Choose the Suggest button.

A list of suggestions appears.

4   Select the word Testing, and then choose the Change button.

The word "Testing" is substituted for the misspelled "Tsting", and the spelling checker moves on to the duplicated word "spelling".

5   Choose the Delete button.

The second instance of "spelling" is deleted. The spelling checker looks through your document until it locates another misspelled or duplicated word, or reaches the end of the document.

6   If the spelling checker locates another spelling error, use the following table to finish checking the spelling of your message.

Use this button	To
Ignore	Ignore only that occurrence of a word.
Ignore All	Ignore all instances of a word in the message.
Change	Change only that occurrence of a word.
Change All	Change all instances of the word in the message.
Add	Add the word to the dictionary for future reference.
Cancel	Cancel the spelling check.
Suggest	Request a list of alternative spellings or words.
Help	Open context-sensitive Help with information about using the spelling checker.

When the spelling checker has checked your entire message, the following dialog box appears:

7   Click OK to close the dialog box telling you that no more misspelled words were found.

Note   You can set an option with the Options command on the Mail menu to run the spelling checker whenever you send a message. If you turn on this option, Microsoft Mail will check the spelling of your messages when you click the Send button.

Sending Messages

Now you are ready to explore some options for sending your messages. To send a message, you can simply click the Send button on the Send Note form as you did before and, in a few moments, your message will arrive at its destination. Or, you can use the Options dialog box for the Send Note form to send messages with special features.

When you send a note through Microsoft Mail, it first goes to the Outbox, where it waits to see if Microsoft Mail is connected to a network. If you are not connected to a network, the message will wait in the Outbox until you are. If you are connected to a network, the message will go to the recipient's Inbox. If you sent copies, the message will also go to those recipients' Inboxes. A copy will also go to your Sent Mail folder for storage, if you have this option turned on. (You will learn about setting options in Lesson 5.)

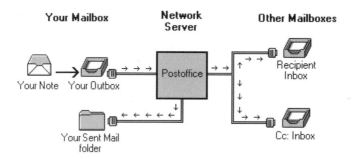

Note   You can send messages to other networks and other mail systems by way of gateways in your Address Book. If you are interested in learning how to work with other mail systems, refer to Appendix D, "Communicating with Other Mail Systems."

Sending Priority Messages

Sometimes you might have an important message that needs more attention than usual. Although most of your messages will be sent with a click of the Send button, you can tag messages with different priorities depending on their importance.

You can choose to send your message with a High, Normal, or Low priority using the Options button on the Send Note form. High priority messages arrive marked with an exclamation point (!) to let the recipient know that the message is important. Normal priority messages are the default setting. Low priority messages arrive with a downward-pointing arrow, indicating that they are less important. The message symbols are shown in the following table.

Symbol	Priority Level
✉ High	High priority
✉	Normal priority
✉ Low	Low priority

Set the message priority

1 Choose the Options button, or press ALT+I.

The Options dialog box opens.

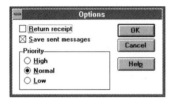

2 In the Priority box, select High and then choose OK.

The Options dialog box closes.

Using Return Receipts

Occasionally, you will have a message that is very important or time sensitive. For these messages, you can request a return receipt that will inform you when the recipient has read your message. You use the Options button to request a return receipt. A return receipt lists who received your message, the subject of the message, the time you composed the message, and the time the addressee read it.

Set the Return Receipt option

1 Choose the Options button.

The Options dialog box opens.

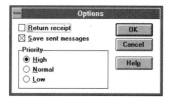

2   In the Options dialog box, click Return Receipt to add an "X" in the check box.

An "X" appears in the Return Receipt check box indicating that this option is selected.

3   Click OK.

The Options dialog box closes.

4   Click the Send button.

Your high priority message is sent. When you read the message, a return receipt will be posted.

One Step Further

If you find yourself sending frequent, similar messages to the same people, you can save yourself some time by composing a pre-addressed message template. To compose a template, you simply compose a new message, fill in the address information and some standard text, and then save the message instead of sending it. You'll learn about sending messages using your template in the next One Step Further.

1   Click the Compose button.

The Send Note form opens.

2   Type **SBS Staff** in the To box.

3   Type **Staff Meeting** in the Subject box.

4   In the text area, type ENTER **AGENDA** ENTER ENTER **REMINDER** ENTER.

These will act as standard headings in your Staff Meeting messages.

5   Double-click the Control-menu box on the Send Note form.

A dialog box opens, asking whether you want to save the changes you made to "Send Note" in the Inbox.

6   Click Yes.

The template is stored in your Inbox but no message is sent at this time. In the One Step Further for Lesson 2, you will open the template, complete the message, and send it.

If You Want to Continue to the Next Lesson

▶ Double-click the Inbox to open it, if it is not already open.

If You Want to Quit Mail for Now

▶ From the File menu, choose Exit And Sign Out.

Lesson Summary

To	Do this
Start Microsoft Mail	Double-click the Microsoft Mail icon, and then enter your name and password.
Compose a new message	Click the Compose button, or press ALT, M, N.
Address a message	Type a name or group name in the To box.
Create a group	From the Mail menu, choose Personal Groups, click New, enter the group name, click Create and select the members, and then choose OK.
Send a Courtesy copy	Type a name or a group name in the Cc box.
Enter message text	Type in the message area.
Edit message text	Type new text at the insertion point, or select text and then press DEL. Choose Cut or Copy and then Paste from the Edit menu to move text around.
Check spelling	From the Edit menu, choose Spelling.
Send a message	Choose the Send button, or press ALT+S.
Compose a message template	Choose the Compose button. Fill in the To and Cc information. Double-click the Control-menu box and press Y to save the template.

For online information about	From the Help menu, choose Contents and then
Addressing a message	Choose "Using the Address Book" and select the topic "Using Mail's Address List" or "Verifying User Names."
Checking spelling	Choose "Sending Messages" and select the topic "Checking Spelling."
Creating groups	Choose "Using the Address Book" and select the topic "Creating or Modifying a Personal Group."
Creating message templates	Choose "Sending Message" and select the topic "Creating and Using a Message Template."

For online information about	From the Help menu, choose Contents and then
Entering and editing text	Choose "Sending Messages" and select the topic "Copying, Moving, or Deleting Information Within a Message."
Sending a message	Choose "Sending Messages" and select the topic "Sending a Message."

For an online demonstration of	From the Help menu, choose Demos and then
Addressing messages	Click the title "Addressing Messages," and then choose the "Keyboard Entry," "Address List," or "Personal Address Book" demonstration.
Checking spelling	Click the title "Composing Messages," and then choose the "Checking Spelling" demonstration.
Creating groups	Click the title "Addressing Messages," and then choose the "Personal Groups" demonstration.
Message templates	Click the title "Addressing Messages," and then choose the "Preaddressed Templates" demonstration.

For more information on	See the *Microsoft Mail User's Guide*
Checking spelling	Chapter 4, "Advanced Features of Mail"
Composing a message	Chapter 3, "Learning Mail—The Basics"
Creating groups	Chapter 3, "Learning Mail—The Basics"
Sending a message	Chapter 3, "Learning Mail—The Basics"

Preview of the Next Lesson

In the next lesson, you'll learn how to find messages that have been sent to you. You can use the Message Finder to locate messages anywhere in your mail box. You will also learn about replying to and forwarding messages, as well as deleting and printing messages.

Receiving Messages

When you receive new messages, Mail can notify you by chiming, by flashing the envelope icon, or both. But what can you do to locate, read, and possibly reply to or forward any specific messages that you have received? And what if you need to print or delete a message? In this lesson, you will learn how to open a folder and read your messages, how to use Message Finder to locate your messages, and how to reply to and forward messages. Then you will explore printing and deleting messages.

You will learn how to:

- Find your messages.
- Reply to a message.
- Forward a message.
- Print and delete messages.

Estimated lesson time: 45 minutes

Start Microsoft Mail

1 Double-click the Microsoft Mail icon.

For information about starting Microsoft Mail, see "Starting Microsoft Mail" in the "Getting Ready" section earlier in this book.

2 Type your name and password, and then press ENTER.

The Microsoft Mail window appears.

3 Click the Maximize button on the Microsoft Mail application window.

To import the practice folder, you must have at least version 3.0b of Microsoft Mail. If you have version 3.0, upgrade it to a later version before continuing with the lessons.

For this lesson, a folder with practice messages has been provided for your use. In order to access the practice messages, you need to import the folder into Microsoft Mail. The next few steps guide you through the importing process.

Import practice messages

1 From the File menu, choose Import Folder.

The Import Folders dialog box opens.

Directories box

2   In the Directories box, double-click the PRACTICE subdirectory of your C:\MSMAIL directory.

3   Select the file EXPORT.MMF, and click OK.

The Import Folders dialog box opens.

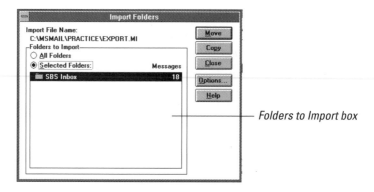

Folders to Import box

4   In the Folders To Import box, select SBS Inbox.

5   Choose the Copy button.

6   Choose the Close button.

Locating and Opening Your Messages

You might have already heard the optional chime that notifies you of new mail, but you might not know where to look for the new message. Or, you might need to refer to a message you sent earlier and might not know whether you have a copy or where a copy resides. Microsoft Mail uses a series of windows and *folders* to organize messages. A folder is simply a holding place for your messages. You will learn more about folders in Lesson 3, "Organizing Your Messages." For now, you need to know that you can find messages in one of four standard storage places—the Inbox, the Sent Mail folder, the Wastebasket, or the Outbox, depending on whether the message is a new incoming message, an old outgoing message, a message that you recently deleted, or a message that you recently sent.

Inbox   The Inbox is a folder that holds any new incoming messages. The Inbox resides in a window that holds other folders, like the Sent Mail folder and the Wastebasket.

Sent Mail   The Sent Mail folder usually holds copies of messages that you have sent to other people. This option can be turned off, as shown in Lesson 5, "Setting Microsoft Mail Options."

Wastebasket   The Wastebasket holds messages you delete. When you quit Mail, they are deleted permanently unless you have changed your options setting. You can permanently delete individual messages from the Wastebasket with the Delete button.

Outbox   The Outbox is a window that acts as a temporary storage area for outgoing messages. If you are working offline (not connected to your network), all messages that you send will wait in the Outbox until you are connected.

Note   If you are working with Microsoft Mail for Windows version 3.1 (the Windows for Workgroups version), you will see a "Deleted Mail folder" in place of the "Wastebasket." These folders function identically, only the name is different between version 3.1 and other versions.

Any of these folders might contain messages that you can open and read. The folder you will work with the most, however, is the Inbox, where all new incoming messages are stored. For many of the exercises in this book, you will use a special folder called SBS Inbox, which has sample messages stored in it, rather than your own Inbox. The SBS Inbox is a folder created for this book, that you imported at the beginning of this lesson.

In practice, new users might have some difficulty distinguishing which folders hold which information. Although the Inbox, Sent Mail, and Wastebasket folders are all part of the same window, the minimized window takes on certain characteristics depending on which folder is active. In the next exercise, you explore the windows and folders that store your messages and learn to recognize the differences between them so that you will be able to find the information you need in each folder more quickly.

Open Mail folders

1   If your Inbox is minimized, double-click the Inbox icon to open it.

The Inbox opens, with a list of folders on the left and a list of messages on the right. Notice that the Sent Mail folder and the Wastebasket are both folders within the same window as the Inbox.

Sent Mail folder (currently closed)

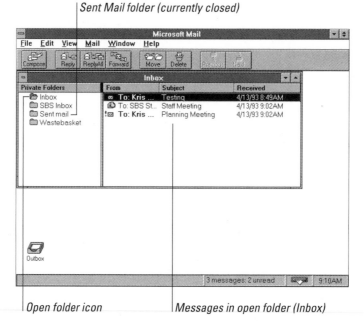

Open folder icon   *Messages in open folder (Inbox)*

2   Double-click the Sent Mail folder.

The Sent Mail folder opens. Remember, the Sent Mail folder holds copies of the messages you sent. You will see the messages you sent earlier.

Name of open folder in title bar

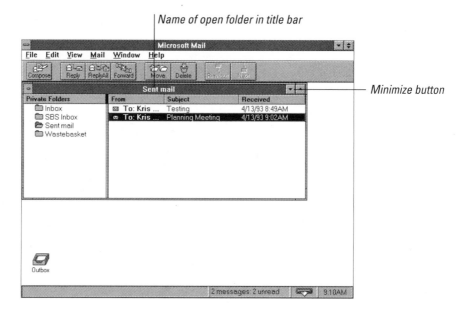

Minimize button

3   In the Sent Mail folder, click the Minimize button.

If the window is maximized, you will need to click the Restore button before you can click the Minimize button. Notice that the minimized Sent Mail folder looks like a file folder, while the minimized Inbox and Outbox both look like a box.

Sent mail

4   Locate and double-click the Outbox icon.

The Outbox is a separate storage area that contains no folders. There are no messages in the Outbox since they have already been sent and copies placed in your Sent Mail folder, if you are connected to a network.

Note   If the Outbox icon is not visible on your screen, choose Arrange Icons from the Window menu to bring it into sight at the bottom of the Microsoft Mail window. Or, choose Outbox from the Window menu to open it.

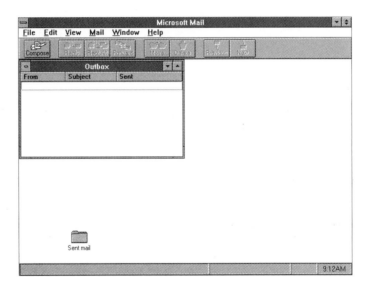

5   Click the Minimize button on the Outbox.

The Outbox is minimized.

6   Double-click the Sent Mail icon.

The Sent Mail folder opens. Notice that although the window is now titled Sent Mail, it still lists the Inbox and other folders on the left side of the window.

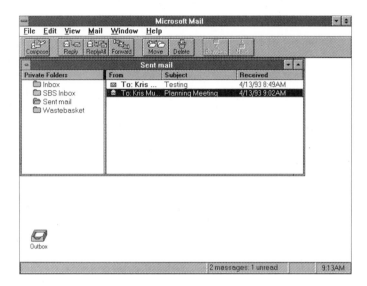

7   Under Private Folders, double-click the Inbox folder.

The Inbox opens, showing all new messages, and the title bar of the window changes from Sent Mail to Inbox.

8   Click the Minimize button on the Inbox.

Inbox

Reading Messages

Now that you know where your incoming messages are stored, how do you open and read them? You can open and read any message in any folder by double-clicking the message. Each message opens in a Read Note form that shows the sender, the recipient(s), the date and time it was sent, and the message itself. You can maximize messages in the Mail application to make them easier to read, or you can minimize messages to get them out of the way while you read others.

In this exercise, as in others in this lesson, you will use the SBS Inbox, a folder with practice messages that were created for this book. Imagine that you are Kris Mueller and that the SBS Inbox is your Inbox, full of messages to read and work with throughout these exercises.

Read messages

1   Double-click the Inbox icon to open the folder window.

2   Under Private Folders, double-click SBS Inbox.

The SBS Inbox opens and shows all of your (Kris Mueller's) incoming messages.

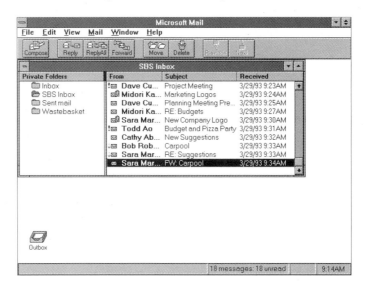

3   Locate the message with the subject "Planning Meeting Presentation" and double-click it.

The message opens.

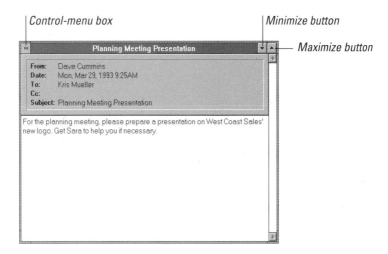

4   Click the Maximize button to maximize the message in Mail, if it is not already maximized.

5   Read through the message.

6   Click the Restore button on the message window.

The message is restored to its original size.

7   Click the Minimize button on the message window.

The message is reduced to an icon at the bottom of the Mail application.

Planning
Meeting
Presentation

Note   The empty envelope icon tells you that the message is open, but minimized.

8   Double-click the message icon for "Planning Meeting Presentation."

The message opens up to its previous size.

9   Double-click the message window Control-menu box.

The message closes.

Reading Return Receipts

You might notice that one of the messages in the list looks a little different than the others. Messages addressed to you with a subject starting with "Registered" are *return receipts*. When you sent the Planning Meeting message, you requested a return receipt. When you read the message, the receipt was sent automatically. To read a return receipt, you simply double-click it just like any other message.

Read a return receipt

1   In the message list, locate the message from Dave Cummins with the subject "Registered: Dave Cummins".

This is a return receipt for a message.

2   Double-click the return receipt message.

The receipt opens.

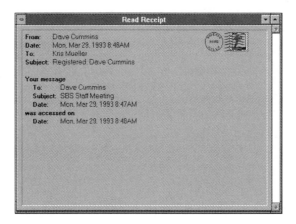

Note   Notice that the return receipt shows who received the message, the date and time it was received, the subject information, and the date and time you sent the message.

3   Double-click the Control-menu box.

The receipt closes.

Using the Message Finder

If you have a lot of messages in your folders, you might have trouble locating the message you want quickly. Mail includes a Message Finder feature that helps you locate exactly the message you want when you specify certain criteria. Message Finder helps you locate messages quickly. All you need to do is tell the Message Finder which message you are looking for and which folders you want to look in, and then press the Start button.

With Message Finder, you can search through messages by sender, subject, recipient, and even by parts of the message text. Using one or more of these criteria, the Message Finder searches through the folders you tell it to look in, and lists the results of its search. In the next exercise, you search for a message from Dave Cummins that includes the word "logo" in its text.

Find a message

1   From the File menu, choose Message Finder.

The Message Finder window opens.

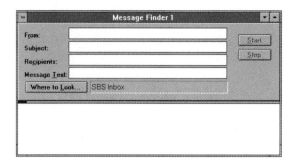

2   In the From box, type **Dave**

3   Move the insertion point to the Message Text area and type **logo**

4   Choose the Where To Look button, and then select "Look in all folders."

5   Choose OK.

6   Choose the Start button, or press ENTER.

All messages with the correct information in your Inbox, SBS Inbox, Sent Mail folder, and Wastebasket appear in a list in the Message Finder.

7   Double-click the "Planning Meeting Presentation" message in the Message Finder list.

The message opens.

8   Double-click the Control-menu box on the message window.

9   Double-click the Control-menu box on the Message Finder window.

The Message Finder closes.

Replying to Messages

Suppose you received a message that required you to reply. If some time has passed between the time you received the message and the time when you have the information you need for a response, the person you respond to might have forgotten the exact nature of the original message. Mail has a Reply feature that can help you with this problem. Instead of composing a new message, filling in the address, subject, and text, and sending your response; you can use the Reply button, or the equivalent Reply command from the Mail menu. When you use the Reply button, a Send Note form opens with the sender's address and the subject automatically filled in, plus the original message appended to the bottom of your reply.

Using the Reply feature can save you quite a bit of time. Since the address and subject are already filled in, you do not have to retype them. Having the original message appended to your reply can also avoid confusion about what you are replying to.

You can use the Reply button to reply only to the person who sent the message, or you can use the Reply All button, and reply to everyone listed in the original Cc box as well. In the next exercise, you reply to the message you sent to yourself in Lesson 1 with the subject "Planning Meeting."

Reply to a message

1   In your own Inbox, double-click to open the "Planning Meeting" message you sent to yourself in Lesson 1.

Note   You can also select the message and click the Reply button, without opening the message.

---

2   With the message open on your Mail workspace, choose the Reply button.

You can also choose the Reply command from the Mail menu, or press CTRL+R. A new Send Note form opens, with the address and subject filled in. The subject is preceded by "RE" for Reply. Notice that the original message text appears at the bottom of the new message.

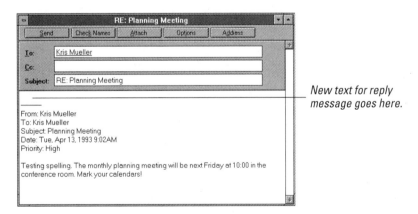

New text for reply message goes here.

3   Type **OK - Working on it!** and then click the Send button.

Your reply is sent back to the original sender, yourself.

Forwarding Messages

Perhaps you received a message from one person that you think another person needs to see. Rather than retyping the message, or showing your copy of the message to the third person, you can use the Forward feature of Microsoft Mail to send the message on to the new recipient. To forward a message to someone without retyping the message, you simply click the Forward button when the message is active and fill in the new address. You can forward a message to several people at a time, and even send courtesy copies, just like any other message. You can also add your own additional comments if you like.

Forward a message

In this exercise, you forward Dave Cummin's message on the subject "Planning Meeting Presentation" to the SBS Staff group.

1 Locate the "Planning Meeting Presentation" message in your SBS Inbox.

2 Double-click the "Planning Meeting Presentation" message to open it.

3 Click the Forward button.

A Send Note form opens with the information about the Planning Meeting Presentation message at the bottom, just like the Reply form. Notice that the subject is preceded by "FW" for Forward.

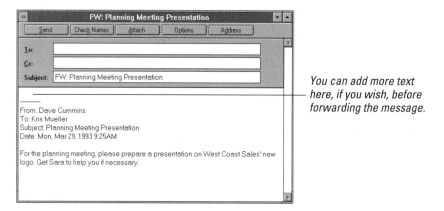

You can add more text here, if you wish, before forwarding the message.

4 In the To box, type **SBS Staff**

Remember, you created the group SBS Staff in Lesson 1. You want this group to receive the "Planning Meeting Presentation" message.

5 Click the Send button.

The message is forwarded to SBS Staff (actually to yourself, since you are the only member of the group).

Note   You can also use the Outbox to forward messages. Simply drag the message to the Outbox, fill in the Send Note form, and then click Send.

Printing and Deleting Messages

If you keep all of the messages that you receive, you'll end up with a very cluttered Mail workspace. You will also use up a lot of your storage space. When you no longer need a message, you should delete it. Deleting messages that you no longer need is easy. You can select the message and then either choose the Delete button from the tool bar, or press DEL, or drag the message from its current folder to the Wastebasket folder.

Sometimes you might want to keep a printed copy of a message. You can print any of the messages that appear in your folders using the Print command from the File menu. You can then delete the message from your folder to conserve storage space.

Print and delete a message

1   In the SBS Inbox folder, select the message about "Planning Meeting Presentation."

2   From the File menu, choose Print.

You do not need to have a message open to print it. You only need to have it selected. The Print dialog box opens.

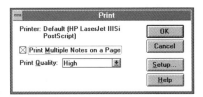

3   If you are attached to a printer, click OK. Otherwise, click Cancel.

Your message prints, if you have an active printer.

4   With the message still selected, choose the Delete button on the tool bar.

The message is moved to the Wastebasket folder, and will be deleted when you quit Mail.

Note   You can also simply drag the message to the Wastebasket and it will be deleted when you quit. Sometimes, if you are moving lots of messages around, it is easier to drag the messages to the Wastebasket than to click the Delete button.

5   Double-click the Wastebasket folder.

The Wastebasket opens with the "Planning Meeting Presentation" message inside.

6   Double-click the SBS Inbox folder.

The Wastebasket folder closes and the SBS Inbox folder opens.

One Step Further

In the One Step Further in Lesson 1, you created a message template with the address, subject, and some text filled in. Templates save you time since you don't need to address them; you simply fill in the text and send it. When you want to use a template, you select it and then click the Forward button. You forward templates rather then send them so that the original template remains intact in your Inbox, ready to use again. You can also drag the template to the Outbox. Either way, the template opens, already addressed, and you can modify the text of the message and send it.

Because you saved the addressed message instead of sending it, you can use the template over and over again without having to delete old information or fill in an address. Try sending a message using the template you created in the last One Step Further.

Use a message template

1   Double-click the Inbox to open it.

2   Select the template with the subject "Staff Meeting," and then click the Forward button.

The Send Note form opens, with the address and subject information filled in already.

3   In the body text area, click in front of the word "AGENDA," and type **The next staff meeting will be Tuesday at 8:30 a.m.** ENTER.

4   Click under the word "AGENDA," and type **Next month's goals** ENTER **Review of last month** ENTER **Other Reports**

5   Click under the word "REMINDER," and type **Check with me about your reports before the meeting.**

6   Click the Send button.

Mail sends the message. Notice that the template remains in your Inbox, ready for you to use again.

If You Want to Continue to the Next Lesson

▶   Double-click your SBS Inbox to open it, if it is not already open.

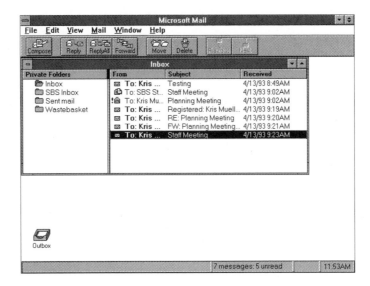

If You Want to Quit Mail for Now

▶ From the File menu, choose Exit And Sign Out.

Lesson Summary

To	Do this
Start Mail	Double-click the Mail icon, and then enter your name and password.
Read a message	Double-click the message.
Find your messages	Choose Message Finder from the File menu, fill in the information you want to search for, and then choose Start.
Reply to a message	Select the message, and then choose the Reply button or press CTRL+R. Type in your comments, and then choose Send.
Forward a message	Select the message, and then choose the Forward button. Type in your comments, and then choose Send.
Use a message template	Select the template, and then choose the Forward button. Fill in the subject, and type your text. Choose the Send button.
Print a message	Select the message, and choose Print from the File menu. Choose OK.

To	Do this
Delete a message	Select the message and then choose the Delete button or press DEL; drag the message to the Wastebasket.

For online information about	From the Help menu, choose Contents and then
Deleting messages	Choose "Working with Messages You've Received" and select the topic "Deleting or Retrieving a Message."
Finding messages	Choose "Working with Messages You've Received" and select the topic "Finding a Message."
Forwarding messages	Choose "Working with Messages You've Received" and select the topic "Forwarding a Message."
Reading messages	Choose "Working with Messages You've Received" and select the topic "Reading a Message."
Replying to messages	Choose "Working with Messages You've Received" and select the topic "Replying to a Message."
Using message templates	Choose "Sending Message" and select the topic "Creating and Using a Message Template."

For an online demonstration of	From the Help menu, choose Demos and then
Deleting messages	Click the title "Managing Messages," and then choose the "Deleting Messages and Folders" demonstration.
Finding messages	Click the title "Finding Messages," and then choose the "Locating Messages" demonstration.
Message templates	Click the title "Addressing Messages," and then choose the "Preaddressed Templates" demonstration.

For more information on	See the *Microsoft Mail User's Guide*
Deleting messages	Chapter 3, "Learning Mail—The Basics"
Finding messages	Chapter 4, "Advanced Features of Mail"
Forwarding messages	Chapter 3, "Learning Mail—The Basics"
Reading messages	Chapter 3, "Learning Mail—The Basics"
Replying to messages	Chapter 3, "Learning Mail—The Basics"
Using message templates	Chapter 4, "Advanced Features of Mail"

Preview of the Next Lesson

In the next lesson, you'll learn how to organize and keep track of your messages by sorting them into folders that you can share or keep private. You will also learn how to arrange the folders themselves so that you can look through them quickly when you need to locate a particular message.

Review & Practice

In the lessons in Part 1, Microsoft Mail Basics, you learned skills to help you compose and send messages, and read, reply to, forward, print, and delete messages. If you want to practice these skills and test your understanding before you proceed with the lessons in Part 2, you can work through the Review & Practice section following this lesson.

Part 1   Review & Practice

Before you move on to Part 2, which covers organizing your messages, attaching files, embedding objects, and setting options, you can practice the skills you learned in Part 1 by working through the steps in this Review & Practice section. You will create a new group, compose a new message, and send it to your new group. Then you find a message, and forward it to a group. Finally, you print and delete the original message.

Scenario

You need to let the accounting department know that the annual budgets must be turned in by Friday, so you'll send a message. Rather than typing the names of the accounting department personnel individually, you decide to create a personal group called SBS Accounting. After you send the message, you receive a message from your supervisor, letting you know that there will also be a pizza party in the conference room when the budgets are turned in. You decide to locate the annual budgets message, add a comment about the pizza party, and forward it to the SBS Accounting group. Then you print the message and finally delete it to conserve storage space.

You will review and practice how to:

- Create a group.
- Compose and address a message.
- Send a message.
- Find and reply to a message.
- Print and delete a message.

Estimated lesson time: 10 minutes

Step 1:   Create a Group

Create a personal group called SBS Accounting. Include yourself.

For more information on	See
Creating groups	Lesson 1

Step 2:   Compose a Message

Compose a new message and address it to the new SBS Accounting group. Add the subject Annual budgets due Friday and type the following text: **Our budget proposals are due Friday. Please send your proposal to me by 4:30 p.m.** Send the message as high priority.

For more information on	See
Composing a message	Lesson 1
Addressing a message	Lesson 1
Entering message text	Lesson 1
Sending a message	Lesson 1

Step 3:   Find and Forward a Message

Locate the message with the subject "Budget and Pizza Party". Select the message and click the Forward button. At the top of the message, add the text: **At 4:30 p.m. there will be a pizza party in the conference room.** Send the message to the SBS Accounting group.

For more information on	See
Finding messages	Lesson 2
Forwarding messages	Lesson 2

Step 4:   Print and Delete a Message

Select the "FW: Budget and Pizza Party" message and print, and then delete the message.

For more information on	See
Printing messages	Lesson 2
Deleting messages	Lesson 2

If You Want to Continue to the Next Lesson

▶ Double-click the Inbox to open it.

If You Want to Quit Mail for Now

▶ From the File menu, choose Exit And Sign Out.

2 Working with Microsoft Mail for Windows

Organizing Messages

This lesson assumes you have set up the practice folder, SBS Inbox, as described in Lesson 2. If you have not done so, go back to the beginning of Lesson 2 and follow the steps under "Import practice messages."

The more messages you receive, the more difficulty you'll have finding the one you want in your Inbox folder. With Microsoft Mail, you can sort messages by several criteria and create special folders for storing messages. In this lesson, you will learn how to manage and organize your messages. You will sort your messages in the message list, create folders to help organize your messages, and arrange the folders so that you can see their contents.

You will learn how to:

- Sort messages.
- Create private folders.
- Move messages between folders.
- Create shared folders.
- Arrange folder windows.

Estimated lesson time: 30 minutes

Start Microsoft Mail

1 Double-click the Microsoft Mail icon.

   For information about starting Microsoft Mail, see "Starting Microsoft Mail" in the "Getting Ready" section earlier in this book.

2 Type your name and password, and then press ENTER.

   The Microsoft Mail window appears.

3 Choose the Maximize button on the Microsoft Mail application window, if it is not already maximized.

Sorting Messages

If you have several messages in your Inbox, finding a particular message can be difficult. Rather than scrolling through your list or using the Message Finder command to locate the message you want, you can use the sort feature to quickly organize your messages.

You can sort your messages by each of four categories listed in the View menu—by Sender, by Date, by Priority, or by Subject. When you sort by sender, your messages are listed in alphabetical order by the name of the person who sent them to you. This order is by first name, if names are entered in *firstname lastname* format in your Mail system. Sorting by Date organizes your messages by the date they were received, starting with the earliest message and ending with the most recent. Sorting by priority gives you the high priority messages at the top of the list and low priority messages at the bottom. Sorting by subject organizes your messages alphabetically by the first letters of the text entered in the subject box. If you press CTRL while choosing any sort command with the mouse, the order of messages is reversed.

Sort messages

1 Double-click the SBS Inbox icon to open this folder.

All messages in the SBS Inbox folder appear in the window.

2 From the View menu, choose Sort By Priority.

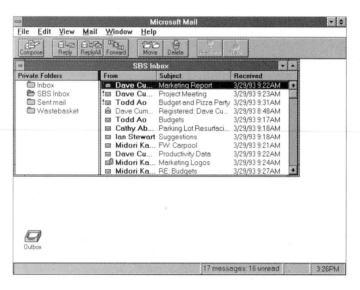

The messages are sorted by priority, with high priority messages at the top and low priority messages at the bottom of the list.

3 From the View menu, choose Sort By Subject.

The messages are rearranged alphabetically according to their subject. Note that the prefixes "RE" for Reply and "FW" for Forward are ignored in the sorting.

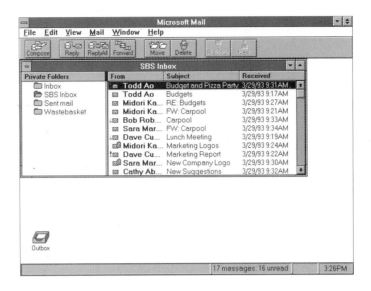

Tip You can also use a shortcut to sort by date received, subject, or sender. Instead of using one of the Sort commands on the View menu, click the header button at the top of the desired column. For example, if you want to sort by date received, click the gray button labeled "Received" and the messages will be sorted by date with the most recent date at the bottom of the list. You can also press CTRL while you click the "Received" button to sort your messages with the most recent date at the top.

Working with Folders

Sometimes, even sorting your messages won't be enough. If you are working on a project and want to keep track of all of the messages related to that project, you can create a special folder to hold only those messages.

You can name new folders anything you like. You can either keep new folders private or share them with others in your mail network, if your administrator has given you that access. You already have a few folders set up when you first start Mail; Inbox, Sent Mail, and Wastebasket are all standard folders. You can decide to use these folders only, or you can create additional folders of your own. For this book, the SBS Inbox folder was specially created to hold your practice messages.

Creating custom folders can help you organize your messages into groups. All messages about budgets, for example, can go into a folder called "Budgets," so you can easily find them. Think of electronic folders as similar to the paper folders in your file cabinet. You can label them by project or by topic, or by whatever best suits your needs.

Creating Private Folders

Private folders are available for your use only, and are not accessible by others on your mail network. To create a new folder, you use the New Folder command on the File menu. When you create a folder, you name it and then choose whether the folder will be a subfolder of an existing folder (such as a folder within the Inbox folder), or a top level folder (a folder that appears in the list at the same level as the Inbox, Sent Mail, and Wastebasket folders).

Create private folders

In this exercise, you create two top-level folders, called Budget and Marketing, and a subfolder under your SBS Inbox folder, called Miscellaneous.

1   Select the first message in your SBS Inbox.

If a folder were selected instead of a message, your new folders would be created as subfolders of the selected folder. You select a message so that your new folders will be top-level folders automatically.

2   From the File menu, choose New Folder.

The New Folder dialog box opens.

3   In the Name box, type **Budget**

This folder will hold all of the budget messages.

4   Choose OK.

Your new folder is created, and appears among the list of Private Folders in the left column.

5   From the File menu, choose New Folder.

The New Folder dialog box opens again.

6   Type **Marketing** and then choose OK.

Another new folder, called Marketing, is created at the top level.

7   From the File menu, choose New Folder.

You will now create a subfolder in your SBS Inbox for miscellaneous messages.

8   Type **Miscellaneous**

9 Choose the Options button.

The New Folder dialog box expands to show additional options.

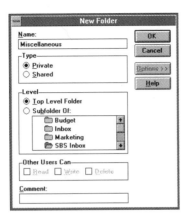

10 Under Level, select Subfolder Of, and then click the SBS Inbox folder.

11 Choose OK.

Your new Miscellaneous folder appears as a subfolder of the SBS Inbox folder.

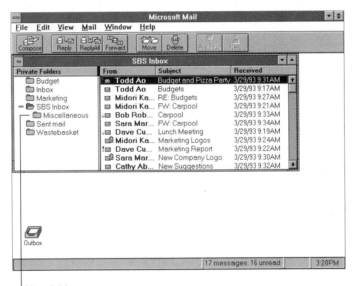

New folder

Moving Messages Between Folders

After you have set up the folders that you want, you can move your messages into them. To move messages, you can simply drag the messages from the folder they are in to the new folder.

Tip   You can move several messages at once if you use the SHIFT and CTRL keys to select them. Hold down SHIFT to select the first and last message in a series, or hold down CTRL to select non-consecutive messages.

Move messages into different folders

1   In the SBS Inbox folder, select the message from Todd Ao with the subject "Budgets".

2   With your mouse, drag the message to the Budget folder in the Private Folders list.

The message disappears from the SBS Inbox folder and moves to the Budget folder.

Note   If you are not using a mouse, you can accomplish the same thing by selecting the message, and then choosing Move from the File menu.

---

3   Locate the "Marketing Report" message from Dave Cummins and drag it to the Marketing folder.

4   Open the Marketing folder to view the message you just moved, and then open SBS Inbox again.

5   Locate the "Lunch Meeting" message from Dave Cummins, and drag it to the Miscellaneous subfolder.

6   Locate the "Suggestions" message from Ian Stewart, and drag it to the Miscellaneous subfolder.

7   Open the Miscellaneous folder.

Your folder should look similar to the following illustration.

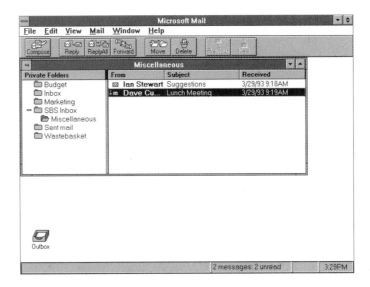

Creating Shared Folders

In addition to private folders, Mail users with proper authorization can create shared folders that are available to others on your network. Your Mail administrator determines who can create and access shared folders. When you set up a new shared folder, you decide whether or not other users can read messages, add messages, or delete messages in the folder.

Note   If you do not have access to shared folders, skip to the next section, "Working With Multiple Folder Windows."

Sharing folders can help on projects when you need to keep information where everyone can access it and when you don't want to generate too many copies of the same messages. With a shared folder, you simply store one copy of a message that others with access privileges can read at their convenience.

Shared folders are not stored in your private mailbox; they are stored in the network postoffice. To view your shared folders, you need to switch from viewing your list of private folders to the list of shared folders.

Create a shared folder

In this exercise, you switch to viewing your list of shared folders, and then create a new shared folder.

1   From the <u>V</u>iew menu, choose <u>S</u>hared Folders.

Shared folders do not appear in the same list as private folders. This command switches between views. The list of shared folders is displayed.

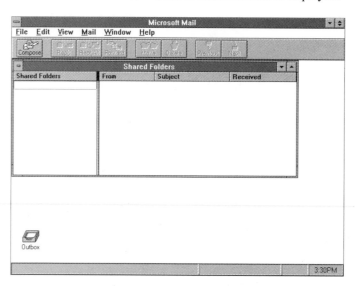

2   Click the View menu.

Notice that the command Shared Folders has changed to Private Folders. With these commands, you can switch back and forth between views.

Tip   You can also click the Private/Shared Folders header button at the top of the list of folders to switch between viewing your lists of private and shared folders.

If someone else has already created a shared folder called "SBS Shared," add a number to the end of your shared folder. For example, use "SBS Shared 1" instead.

3   From the <u>F</u>ile menu, choose <u>N</u>ew Folder.

The New Folder dialog box opens.

4   Type **SBS Shared** and then click the Options button.

5   Under Type, select Shared.

6   Under Level, select Top Level Folder.

7   Choose OK.

Your new shared folder, SBS Shared, appears in the list of shared folders. Other shared folders created by your administrator might also be listed.

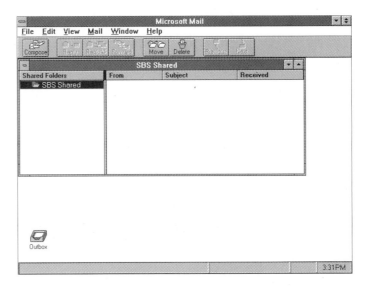

8   From the <u>V</u>iew menu, choose Private <u>F</u>olders, or click the Shared Folders header button.

Working with Multiple Folder Windows

Suppose you want to view lists of messages in two folders at the same time, for example, to check for messages with similar dates or topics. A folder window, however, can only display a message list from one folder at a time. Fortunately, you can open a new, second window and arrange your desktop so that two different folders are visible. The Window menu has commands that open a new window and arrange your windows in one of two ways—*cascaded* or *tiled*. When you choose the Cascade command, the windows are stacked on top of each other in a staggered way so that you can see the title bars of each window and the contents of the top window. When you choose the Tile command, the windows are arranged horizontally so that you can see the contents of both windows.

In the next exercise, you will create a new window and a new folder, arrange the windows so that you can see the messages in two different folders, and then move a message from one window to the other.

Arrange two folder windows

1   Open the SBS Inbox folder.

2   From the <u>W</u>indow menu, choose <u>N</u>ew Window.

A new window opens, displaying the same folders as your existing window.

3   From the <u>F</u>ile menu, choose <u>N</u>ew Folder.

4   Type **SBS Extra** and then click OK.

5   In the new window, open the SBS Extra folder.

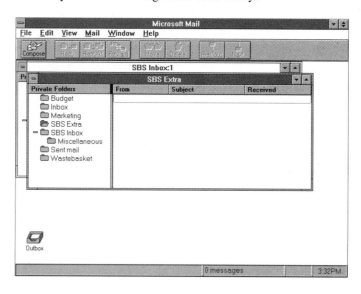

6   From the Window menu, choose Cascade.

The windows rearrange so that you can see the title bar of each window, but the contents of only the top one. Cascading is most useful when you are working with several windows. When the windows are cascaded, you can always select the window you need and bring it into view easily.

7 From the Window menu, choose Tile.

The windows rearrange so that you can see both the title bars and the contents of each window. Tiling is most useful when you have only two windows open, as in this case.

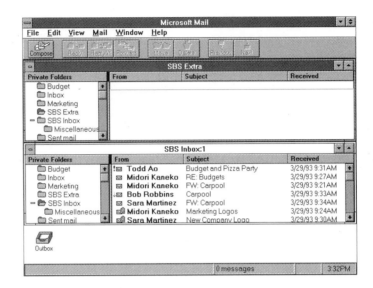

8 In the SBS Inbox window, select the "New Suggestions" message from Cathy Abdul.

If necessary, scroll down to bring the message into view.

9 Drag the "New Suggestions" message to the folder called SBS Extra in the left column of the other window.

Your new folder now contains the "New Suggestions" message.

You can move several messages at once if you use the SHIFT and CTRL keys to select them. Hold down SHIFT to select the first and last message in a series, or hold down CTRL to select non-consecutive messages.

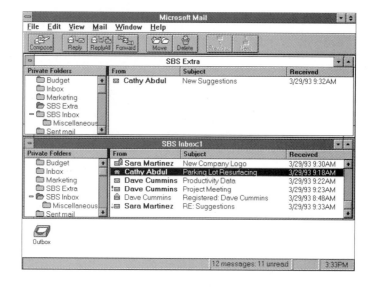

Tip   Use this two-window technique to move messages between private and shared folders. Display private folders in one window and shared folders in another.

Deleting Folders

You can delete folders in the same way that you delete messages, by clicking the Delete button on the tool bar. Because folders often hold several messages, a dialog box opens when you click the Delete button to verify that you want to delete the folder and all messages inside it. In this exercise, you will delete the SBS Extra folder you created earlier and the New Suggestions message inside it, and then close the second folder window.

Delete a folder

1   In the list of folders in either window, select the SBS Extra folder.

2   Choose the Delete button on the tool bar.

A dialog box opens, asking if you want to delete the folder and any messages inside.

3   Choose Yes.

4 On one of the folder windows, double-click the Control-menu box.

The window closes.

5 From the <u>W</u>indow menu, choose <u>T</u>ile.

The remaining window is arranged to fill most of the Microsoft Mail window.

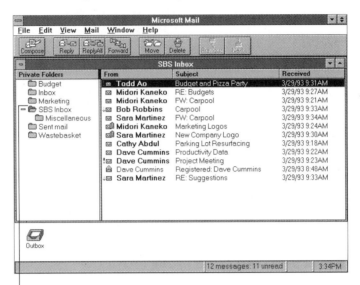

If there was an existing "SBS Shared" folder, be sure you delete the folder you created, "SBS Shared 1."

| *Note that the SBS Extra folder has been deleted.*

6 If you have access to shared folders, switch to your shared folder list and delete the folder named SBS Shared that you created earlier in this lesson, then switch back to private folders.

One Step Further

You've learned to create folders and to move messages into them to organize your messages. Perhaps you have a folder for a project that you haven't worked on in a few days. You might need to review all of the messages to see if there is something that you need to check on or complete. You can open each individual message, read it, and then close it, or you can use the Previous and Next buttons on the tool bar to move through the messages more quickly. Try moving the "Budgets" and "Marketing Report" messages into the Miscellaneous folder, read through the messages in the Miscellaneous folder using the Next and Previous buttons, and then delete the "Lunch Meeting" message using the Delete button.

1 Move the "Budgets" message from the Budget folder to the Miscellaneous folder and the "Marketing Report" message from the Marketing folder to the Miscellaneous folder.

2 Open the Miscellaneous folder and open the "Budgets" message.

3 Use the Next button to open the "Lunch Meeting" message.

4 Use the Next button to open the "Marketing Report" message.

5 Use the Previous button to return to the "Lunch Meeting" message.

6 With the message open, use the Delete button to delete the message.

Notice that when you delete an open message, the current message disappears and the next message in the list opens.

7 Close the message.

If You Want to Continue to the Next Lesson

▶ Double-click the SBS Inbox to open it, if it is not already open.

If You Want to Quit Mail for Now

▶ From the File menu, choose Exit And Sign Out.

Lesson Summary

To	Do this
Sort messages	Choose Sort By Sender, Subject, Date, or Priority from the View menu.
Create a new folder	Choose New Folder from the File menu, type the name, choose Private or Shared, choose Options and choose a level. Choose OK.
Move a message	Drag the message from the old folder to the new folder.
Arrange windows	Choose New Window from the Window menu, and then choose Tile or Cascade from the Window menu.
Delete a folder	Choose the Delete button from the toolbar. Choose Yes to delete the folder and all messages inside.

For online information about	From the Help menu, choose Contents and then
Creating folders	Choose "Using Folders" and select the topic "Creating a Folder or Subfolder."
Moving messages	Choose "Using Folders" and select the topic "Moving Messages Between Folders."

For an online demonstration of	From the Help menu, choose Demos and then
Creating folders	Click the title "Managing Messages," and then choose the "Creating Private Folders," or the "Creating Shared Folders" demonstration.
Moving messages	Click the title "Managing Messages," and then choose the "Moving Messages" demonstration.
Sorting messages	Click the title "Finding Messages," and then choose the "Collecting Special Messages" demonstration.

For more information on	See the *Microsoft Mail User's Guide*
Using folders	Chapter 4, "Advanced Features of Mail"

Preview of the Next Lesson

In the next lesson, you'll learn how to attach files to, and embed objects in, your messages. You can attach any kind of file to a message, and the recipients can save the attached file to their own disks. You can even view embedded objects right in the message.

Attaching Files and Embedding Objects

If you've been working on a file and you need to give it to someone else for review, you would usually print the file and deliver it in paper form. Microsoft Mail for Windows can save you time and paper, however, by letting you attach files to, and embed objects in, your messages. Rather than print a file and deliver it physically, you can attach the file to a message and send the two together through the network. Or, you can embed the information in your message so that it is visible when the message is displayed. In this lesson, you will explore attaching files to and embedding objects in your messages. You will also learn to save attached files on your own hard disk.

You will learn how to:

- Attach files to messages.
- View and save attached files.
- Embed objects in messages.

Estimated lesson time: 35 minutes

Start Microsoft Mail

1   Double-click the Microsoft Mail icon.

For information about starting Microsoft Mail, see "Starting Microsoft Mail" in the "Getting Ready" section earlier in this book.

2   Type your name and password, and then press ENTER.

The Microsoft Mail window appears.

3   Click the Maximize button on the Microsoft Mail application window, if it is not already maximized.

Attaching Files

When you work with others on a project, you often share files back and forth while members of the team make their contributions or comment on the progress. In order to make such file sharing a little easier, Mail allows you to *attach* files to your messages. When you attach a file, a copy of the file is "paper-clipped" to your message. The file travels through the network with your message. When the recipients open their messages, they can open and save the attached file to their networks or hard disks.

You can attach files to a message by choosing the Attach button in the Send Note form. A dialog box opens that lets you select files to attach. You can attach almost any kind of file: spreadsheets, word processing documents, pictures, batch files, programs, or any other file that you can store on your computer.

When you attach a file, Mail makes a copy of it and sends the copy with your message so that the original file remains intact. An attached file appears as an icon in the body of your message, with the file name below the icon. In this exercise, you attach a graphic file to a message, and then send it to yourself.

Attach a file

1   Choose the Compose button on the tool bar.

The Send Note form opens.

2   In the To box, type your name, and then press TAB twice.

3   In the Subject box, type **New Marketing Program** and then press TAB.

4   In the body area, type **Here is a graphic for the new marketing program**.

Your message should look like the following:

Attach button

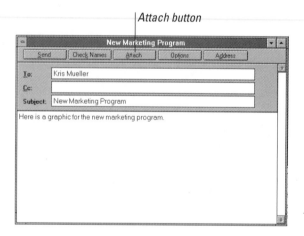

5   Choose the Attach button, or press ALT+A.

The Attach dialog box opens.

File Name box   Directories box

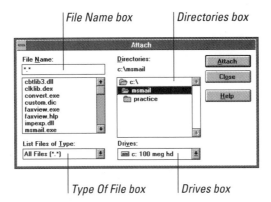

Type Of File box   Drives box

6   In the Drives box, select your hard disk (usually drive C).

7   In the Directories box, double-click the PRACTICE subdirectory under the MSMAIL directory.

8   In the File Name list box, select MARKET.BMP.

9   Choose the Attach button in this dialog box, and then choose Close.

The file is attached and an icon representing the attached file appears in your message text.

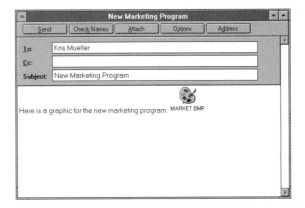

10   Choose the Send button.

Your message and its attachment are sent.

Viewing Attached Files

You view an attached file by opening the message, and then opening the attachment. An attached file is separate from your message, although it is sent through Mail with the message. In order to open an attached file, you need to have the application it was created in installed on your computer. To open an attached file, you simply double-click the icon. If you do not have the application that the attached file was created in, you cannot view the attachment. In this exercise, you view an attached graphics file in Windows Paintbrush, a painting application that comes with Microsoft Windows.

View an attached file

1 In your SBS Inbox, locate the message from Midori Kaneko with the subject "Marketing Logos".

This is a message with a file attached to it. Notice that the message icon looks like it has a file paper-clipped to it.

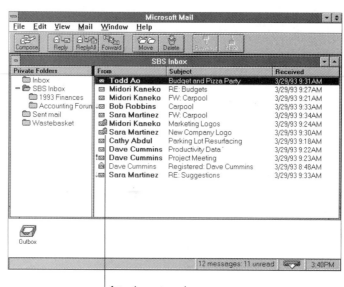

Attachment marker

2 Double-click the message to open it.

Notice the icon in the text for the attached file.

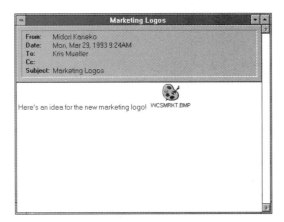

3   Double-click the file icon in the message body text.

Paintbrush starts with the file WCSMRKT.BMP open.

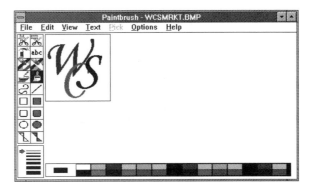

4   Look over the graphic, and then double-click the Paintbrush Control-menu box to close Paintbrush.

5   Double-click the Control-menu box on the message to close it.

Saving Attached Files

Suppose you have a message that includes an attached file that you often need to use. You can save the attached file to your own hard disk rather than keeping the message in your Inbox and opening it every time you need the file. When you save an attached file to your own hard disk, you can use it any time, regardless of whether you are running Mail or whether you have that particular message open. In this exercise, you save an attached file to your hard disk.

Save an attached file

1 Open the "Marketing Logos" message again.

You must open the message containing the attachment before you can save it.

2 Click once to select the attached file icon (but don't open the file).

3 From the File menu, choose Save Attachment.

The Save Attachment dialog box opens.

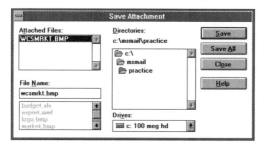

4 In the Directories box, double-click C:\, and then double-click MSMAIL.

Note The standard installation of Microsoft Mail for Windows creates the MSMAIL Directory. If you changed the name of that directory, or placed your MSMAIL files in another directory, use that directory instead of MSMAIL in these exercises.

5 Choose the Save button.

6 Choose the Close button.

The Save Attachment dialog box closes. Now you can use File Manager or the application that the file was created in to open the file.

7 Double-click the Control-menu box on the message.

The message closes.

Embedding Objects

Suppose you have been working on some numbers in a spreadsheet or some text in a word processing document. If you want to send the information to someone else without attaching a separate file or retyping everything, you can *embed* it into your message.

Embedded objects, unlike attached files, are not separate documents. They become an integral part of your message. When you attach a file, you choose the file you want and attach it to your message. When you embed an object in a message, however, you copy the object from the original application and paste it into your message.

Remember that attached files are completely separate files, sent with the message, while embedded objects are part of the message.

After you embed an object, you do not need to open any separate files to see it or to edit it. Unlike attached files, you view the object right in your Mail message. You can also double-click the object to edit it if you have the original application.

To send an embedded object with your message, you create a new message and then switch to the application that the object is in. You then copy the object from the application, switch back to Mail, and paste the object into your message, as in the next exercises.

Create a new message

1   Choose the Compose button.

The Send Note form opens.

2   In the To box, type your name, and then press TAB twice.

You will send your message and the embedded file to yourself.

3   In the Subject box, type **New Marketing Logo** and then press TAB.

4   In the body area, type **Here is the new logo for the Marketing department. Tell me what you think:**

Copy an object to embed

1   Click the Minimize button for the Microsoft Mail application window.

2   In the Program Manager, locate the Paintbrush icon.

It is often found in the Accessories group and looks like this:

3   Double-click the Paintbrush icon to open it.

Paintbrush

Paintbrush opens.

4   From the File menu, choose Open.

The Open dialog box appears.

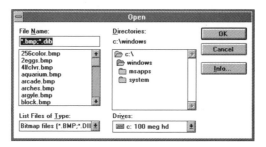

5   In the Drives box, select drive C.

6   In the Directories box, double-click C:\ , double-click MSMAIL, and then double-click PRACTICE.

7   In the list of files, double-click LOGO.BMP.

The picture file LOGO.BMP opens.

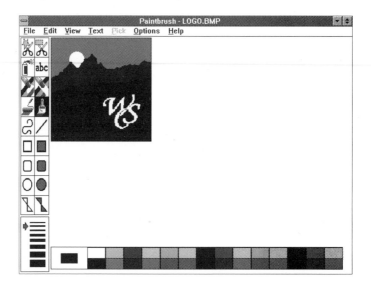

8   Choose the Pick tool.

It looks like this.

9   Drag from the upper-left corner of the logo to the bottom-right corner to select the entire image.

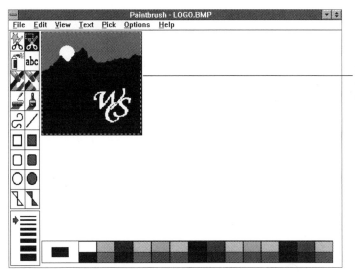

Dotted line surrounding selected picture area

10   From the Edit menu, choose Copy.

11   Double-click the Control-menu box on Paintbrush.

Paintbrush closes.

Embed an object

1   Double-click the Microsoft Mail icon that is minimized at the bottom of your screen.

Mail is restored to its original size.

2   In your "New Marketing Logo" message, place your insertion point at the end of the text.

3   From the Edit menu, choose Paste Special.

The Paste Special dialog box opens. Using Paste Special instead of Paste lets you specify what kind of object you are pasting, and allows you to be sure that the formatting is saved when the object is pasted.

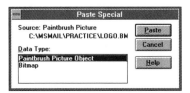

4   Select Paintbrush Picture Object, and then choose the Paste button.

The Paintbrush object is pasted into your document.

5   Choose the Send button.

Viewing Embedded Objects

Remember, embedded objects, unlike attached files, are part of your message. You do not need the application that the object was created in to view the object. You simply need to open the message to view the embedded object. In the next exercise, you open a practice message from the SBS Inbox and view an embedded object.

View an embedded object

1   In your SBS Inbox, locate the message with the subject "New Company Logo".

Note   Messages with embedded objects are marked with the same "paper clip" marker as messages with attachments.

---

2   Open the message.

The message opens with the embedded object visible.

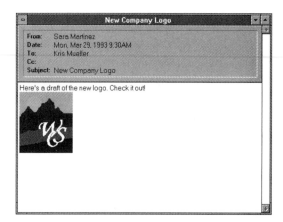

3   Double-click the Control-menu box on the message window.

The message closes.

One Step Further

You've seen how to attach a file to a message, send it, and then save the attached file. You can also edit an attached file and save the changes to it, just like any other file. Editing an attached file changes only the copy in the message, not the copy on your hard disk. Try attaching a text file instead of a graphic, editing it, and then saving it in the message.

1   Compose a new message to SBS Staff with the subject "Marketing Memo" and attach the file MEMO.WRI from your PRACTICE directory.

2   Open MEMO.WRI and add your name above the date.

3   Save the changes to MEMO.WRI and close the application.

4   Close the message and choose Yes to save changes.

5   Open the message from your Inbox and open the attached file to verify that the changes were saved.

6   Close the memo and the Mail message.

If You Want to Continue to the Next Lesson

Minimize the Inbox

▶   Choose the Minimize button on the Inbox.

If You Want to Quit Mail for Now

▶   From the File menu, choose Exit And Sign Out.

Lesson Summary

To	Do this
Attach a file	In the Send Note form, choose the Attach button, select the file, and then choose Attach. Choose Close and send the file.
Save an attached file	Open the message. Choose Save Attachment from the File menu. Select the directory you want, and then choose Save. Choose Close.
Embed an object	Open the application that you want to copy the object from. Select the object and choose Copy from the Edit menu. Create a new message in Mail, and choose Paste Special from the Edit menu. Select the type of object, and then choose OK.

For online information about	From the Help menu, choose Contents and then
Attaching files	Choose "Including Files and Objects in Messages" and select the topic "Attaching a File."
Embedding objects	Choose "Including Files and Objects in Messages" and select the topic "Embedding an Object in a Message" or "Working with an Embedded Object."
Saving attached files	Choose "Including Files and Objects in Messages" and select the topic "Opening and Saving an Attachment."

For an online demonstration of	**From the Help menu, choose Demos and then**
Attaching files	Click the title "Composing Messages," and then choose the "Attaching Files" demonstration.
Embedding objects	Click the title "Composing Messages," and then choose the "Inserting Objects" demonstration.
Saving attached files	Click the title "Composing Messages," and then choose the "Working With Attached Files" demonstration.

For more information on	**See the *Microsoft Mail User's Guide***
Attaching files	Chapter 4, "Advanced Features of Mail"
Embedding objects	Chapter 4, "Advanced Features of Mail"

Preview of the Next Lesson

In the next lesson, you'll learn how to customize Mail by setting options in the Options dialog box and how to change your password to protect your messages.

Setting Microsoft Mail Options

When you install Mail, certain options are automatically set. These options are called *defaults*. While you might find these default settings helpful, you might want to change some of them. By changing options, you can set Mail to look for new messages at certain intervals, save copies of messages that you send, or even automatically check the spelling in your messages before they are sent. You can also change your password to protect your messages from others. In this lesson, you will learn how to customize Mail with various option settings, and then learn to set your password.

You will learn how to:

- Set Mail options.

- Change your password.

Estimated lesson time: 20 minutes

Start Microsoft Mail

1   Double-click the Microsoft Mail icon.

For information about starting Microsoft Mail, see "Starting Microsoft Mail" in the "Getting Ready" section earlier in this book.

2   Type your name and password, and then press ENTER.

The Microsoft Mail window appears.

3   Click the Maximize button on the Microsoft Mail application window, if it is not already maximized.

Setting Message Options

Perhaps you want Mail to check the spelling of your messages automatically before they are sent. Or perhaps you don't want to delete messages from the Wastebasket automatically when you quit Mail. You can set options for many things in Microsoft Mail for Windows. Some of the most useful options control how Mail sends your messages and how it notifies you of new messages. In the next exercise, you will set a few of the options in the Options dialog box.

Set Mail options

1   From the Mail menu, choose Options.

The Options dialog box opens.

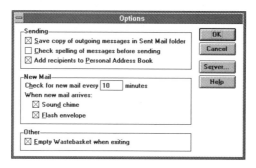

2 In the Sending box, check to see if the "Save copy of outgoing messages in Sent Mail folder" option is selected.

3 If the option is not selected, click the check box to select it. If it is selected, go to step 4.

When "Save copy of outgoing messages in Sent Mail folder" is selected, Mail saves a copy of every message you send so you can refer to it later. If you clear the check box, Mail will not retain copies of your sent messages.

Note All of the options with check boxes are toggle switches. Toggle switches can be turned either on or off. If the switch is on (the option is selected), and you click the box, the switch will be turned off, and vice versa.

---

4 In the Sending box, check to see whether the "Check spelling of outgoing messages before sending" check box is selected.

Note If you are using Microsoft Mail version 3.1 (the Windows for Workgroups version), you will not have the "Check spelling" option. Skip to step 6.

---

5 If the check box is selected, go on to step 6. If not, click the box to select the option.

Now the spelling checker will automatically check your messages when you send them.

6 In the New Mail box, select the contents of the "minutes" box and then type **5**

This tells Mail to look for new messages every 5 minutes.

7 In the New Mail box, check to see if the "Sound chime" option is selected.

The chime function might work differently in different installations.

8 If the check box is clear, click the "Sound chime" check box to select it. If it is selected, go to step 9.

This option is turned on. When this option is on and Mail is running, your computer makes a sound to notify you when you get a new message.

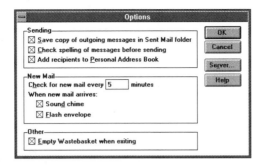

For more information about the options you did not change in this exercise, refer to the "Setting Mail Options" topic in Help.

Note   If you clear the "Empty Wastebasket when exiting" option, your deleted messages will remain in your Wastebasket until you delete them individually from that folder.

---

9   Click the OK button.

The Options dialog box closes with your new settings saved.

Checking the Effects of Changing Options

Now that you've set some options, you can see the results. In the next exercise, you will create a new message and send it to yourself so you can see your options in action.

Create and send a new message

1   Choose the Compose button.

The Send Note form opens.

2   In the To box, type your name.

3   In the Subject box, type **Testing Options**

4   In the text area, type **When I send this message, the spelling will be checked automatically and a chime will sound when the message arrives in my Inbox.**

Don't bother to correct any typos you might make while typing in the text; let the spelling checker find them.

5   Choose Send.

The Spelling dialog box opens. Correct any typos that are detected, as you learned to do in Lesson 1.

Note If you are using Microsoft Mail version 3.1 (the Windows for Workgroups version), you will not have the "Check spelling" option. Skip to step 7.

6 At the word "Inbox", choose Ignore.

The message is sent. After a few moments, a chime sounds to notify you that you have new mail.

Note If there are more misspelled words, use the Ignore, Ignore All, Change, Change All, Suggest, or Add button to correct the problem.

7 Double-click the Inbox folder to open it, if necessary.

8 Open the new "Testing Options" message.

If the message has not arrived yet, wait a few moments. Because you set the "Sound Chime" option, you will hear a chime when the message arrives.

9 Double-click the Control-menu box on the message to close it.

10 Double-click the Sent Mail folder to open it.

Because you set the "Save copy of outgoing messages in Sent Mail folder" option, you should see another copy of the "Testing Options" message in your Sent Mail folder.

Changing Your Password

If you have just installed Mail and your password is set to the default ("PASS-WORD"), or if you suspect someone else knows your password, you should change your password to protect your messages. If others know your password, they can open your mailbox and read your messages. You should never tell anyone else your password if you want your messages to remain private.

If you forget your password, see your system administrator.

You can change your password while you are working in Microsoft Mail with the Change Password command on the Mail menu. Passwords can be any word or combination of letters and numbers, up to eight characters long. You can use upper-case or lowercase letters. When you set your password, you should change it to something unique that you can easily remember.

Password length	Allowable characters
Up to 8 characters	1234567890
	abcdefghijklmnopqrstuvwxyz
	ABCDEFGHIJKLMNOPQRSTUVWXYZ

Tip   Choose a password that is easy to remember, but not one that can easily be guessed. Do not use your name or your phone extension, for example.

Change your password

1   From the <u>M</u>ail menu, choose <u>C</u>hange Password.

The Change Password dialog box appears.

2   In the Old Password box, type your current password, and then press TAB.

3   In the New Password box, type **mail**, and then press TAB.

This tells Microsoft Mail for Windows that you want to set your password to "MAIL".

Warning   If you press ENTER instead of TAB in step 3, you will set your password to the ENTER key. If you accidentally press ENTER, you will need to change your password again from ENTER to a word.

4   In the Verify New Password box, type **mail** again, and then click OK.

You must verify the new password before Microsoft Mail for Windows will change it. When you click OK, Mail checks the new password and the verification, and then changes your password.

Note   If the dialog box does not close when you press ENTER, you might have misspelled the new password in the Verify New Password box, or the old password in the Old Password box. Try retyping the passwords, and then press ENTER again.

5   Click OK at the confirmation box.

Restore your password to the original

1   From the Mail menu, choose Change Password.

2   In the Old Password box, type **mail**

Note   When you change your password permanently, be sure to use a password more unique and secure than the example password "mail".

---

3   In the New Password box, type your original password.

4   In the Verify New Password box, type your original password again.

5   Click OK.

Your password is restored to its original setting.

One Step Further

You can change most of your Microsoft Mail for Windows settings using the menu, but there are some options that you can only change in a special text file called MSMAIL.INI, which is used by Microsoft Windows to store certain setting for the Mail program. You can use the MSMAIL.INI file to set some additional options, such as changing the security level so that others cannot easily view your messages.

If you feel comfortable changing files such as an INI file, follow the steps below to make Microsoft Mail for Windows more secure. First you will make a backup copy of your MSMAIL.INI file. Then you will change some settings in your active MSMAIL.INI file. With the SECURITY=1 command, you set Microsoft Mail so that you will have to enter your password whenever you restore it from a minimized icon.

Back up your MSMAIL.INI file

1   Quit Mail, and then switch to Program Manager and locate the Notepad program icon.

The MSMAIL.INI file controls how Microsoft Mail for Windows will appear when it starts. You need to quit Mail before changing the INI file so that you can see the effects when you restart. The Notepad icon looks like this:

Notepad

2   Double-click the Notepad icon to open it.

Notepad is an editing program, similar to a word processor, which is designed to work on relatively small text files such as this one.

3 From the File menu, choose Open.

The Open dialog box appears.

4 Under Drives, select drive C, and then, under Directories, double-click WIN-DOWS.

5 In the List Files of Type box, select All Files (*.*).

6 In the File Name list, scroll down until you locate MSMAIL.INI and select it.

7 Choose OK.

The MSMAIL.INI file opens. It should look something like this:

Warning Be very careful whenever you open or change the MSMAIL.INI file. If you are not sure of what a command in the file does, do not alter the command. This file controls how your copy of Microsoft Mail for Windows behaves, so be sure you understand what you are changing before you do it.

---

8 From the File menu, choose Save As.

You will save a backup copy of your MSMAIL.INI file with a different name.

9 Type **1msmail.bak** and then choose OK.

Your backup file is saved.

Change your MSMAIL.INI file

1 From the File menu, choose Open.

The Open dialog box appears again.

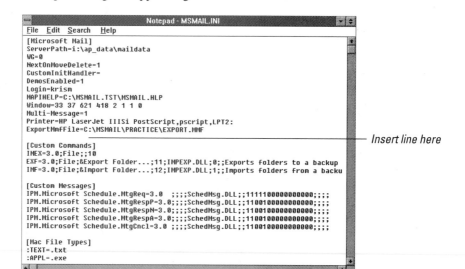

```
                        Notepad - MSMAIL.INI
 File  Edit  Search  Help
[Microsoft Mail]
ServerPath=i:\ap_data\maildata
WG=0
NextOnMoveDelete=1
CustomInitHandler=
DemosEnabled=1
Login=krism
MAPIHELP=C:\MSMAIL.TST\MSMAIL.HLP
Window=33 37 621 418 2 1 1 0
Multi-Message=1
Printer=HP LaserJet IIISi PostScript,pscript,LPT2:
ExportMmFFile=C:\MSMAIL\PRACTICE\EXPORT.MMF

[Custom Commands]
IMEX=3.0;File;;10
EXF=3.0;File;&Export Folder...;11;IMPEXP.DLL;0;;Exports folders to a backup
IMF=3.0;File;&Import Folder...;12;IMPEXP.DLL;1;;Imports folders from a backu

[Custom Messages]
IPM.Microsoft Schedule.MtgReq=3.0  ;;;;SchedMsg.DLL;;1111100000000000;;;;
IPM.Microsoft Schedule.MtgRespP=3.0;;;;SchedMsg.DLL;;1100100000000000;;;;
IPM.Microsoft Schedule.MtgRespN=3.0;;;;SchedMsg.DLL;;1100100000000000;;;;
IPM.Microsoft Schedule.MtgRespA=3.0;;;;SchedMsg.DLL;;1100100000000000;;;;
IPM.Microsoft Schedule.MtgCncl=3.0 ;;;;SchedMsg.DLL;;1100100000000000;;;;

[Mac File Types]
:TEXT=.txt
:APPL=.exe
```

Insert line here

2 In the Files list, scroll down until you locate MSMAIL.INI and select it.

3 Choose OK.

The MSMAIL.INI file opens again.

4 Use the mouse or the DOWN ARROW key to move down to the bottom of the first section of text, and then type **SECURITY=1** and press ENTER.

5 From the File menu, choose Save.

6 From the File menu, choose Exit.

Notepad closes.

7 Restart Mail, and then minimize it.

8 Double-click the minimized icon.

A dialog box opens, asking for your password.

9 Type your password and press ENTER.

Mail opens.

> **Note** If you want to remove the extra security from your MSMAIL.INI file, simply open the file in Notepad again, and change the 1 to 0 or delete the SECURITY=1 line completely. For more information about other settings you can change in your MSMAIL.INI file, look in the Help system under MSMAIL.INI or Configuration File Entries.

If You Want to Continue to the Next Lesson

▶ Double-click the Inbox to open it.

If You Want to Quit Mail for Now

▶ From the File menu, choose Exit And Sign Out.

Lesson Summary

To	Do this
Set options	Choose Options from the Mail menu, select the options you want, and then click OK.
Change your password	Choose Change Password from the Mail menu. Type the old password, TAB, type the new password, TAB, type the new password again, and then press ENTER.

For online information about	From the Help menu, choose Contents and then
Changing your password	Choose "Getting Started with Mail" and select the topic "Changing Your Password."
Setting options	Choose "Setting Mail Options."

Preview of the Next Lesson

In the next lesson, you will learn how to import and export message files so that you can take your messages with you when you travel or work at home.

Importing and Exporting Message Files

Suppose you are going on a business trip, or home to work for a day, and you need to send some Microsoft Mail for Windows messages about your work as soon as you get back. While you are away, you could create some paper reminders about the messages you want to send. Or, if you have a portable computer, you could draft them with your word processor. The most efficient approach, however, is to *export* a message file, work on your messages with Microsoft Mail installed on your home or portable computer, and then *import* your revised message file when you return to the office.

In this lesson, you will move messages into a new folder to export, create an export file that includes the new folder, and then import a message file to your computer.

You will learn how to:

- Create an export message file.
- Import a message file.

Estimated lesson time: 25 minutes

Start Microsoft Mail for Windows

1   Double-click the Microsoft Mail icon.

For information about starting Microsoft Mail, see the "Getting Ready" section earlier in this book.

2   Type your name and password, and then press ENTER.

The Microsoft Mail window appears.

3   Click the Maximize button on the Microsoft Mail application window, if it is not already maximized.

Creating an Export File

Before you leave on your business trip or your day of working at home, you want to be sure that you'll have all of the tools you need. If you plan to work with any mail messages that were sent to you (if you need to send replies after doing some research, for example), you'll need to take these messages along. While you can always print them and refer to the paper copy, you can also create an *export file* with the messages you need, and use that on your laptop or home computer.

An export file contains one or more folders with messages in them, as well as a copy of your Personal Address Book so that you can still address your messages even if you're away from the network. When you create your export file, you specify which folders from your mailbox you want to export. Then you can create the export file in one of two ways: You can either copy your folders, so that you have a backup when you return, or you can move them off the system completely. You can copy or move any of your folders onto a hard disk or floppy disk, as long as you have enough room on your disk.

The SBS Inbox folder that you have been using for some of the lessons was created this way, by copying a folder into an export file. In the next exercise, you will set up a folder with some messages in it, and then create an export file containing a copy of that folder.

Create a new folder

1   From the File menu, choose New Folder.

The New Folder dialog box opens.

2   In the Name box, type **SBS Export** and then click the Options button.

The dialog box expands to show several options.

3   In the Level box, click the Top Level Folder option.

4   Click OK.

The New Folder dialog box closes and your new folder, SBS Export, appears in your list of folders.

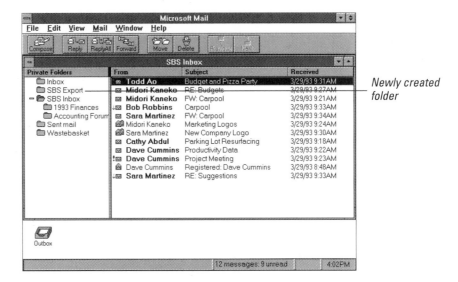

Newly created
folder

5   Double-click the SBS Inbox folder.

The SBS Inbox folder opens.

6   Holding down CTRL, select all of the messages with the word "Carpool" in the
subject box.

7   Drag the selected messages over to the SBS Export folder in the folders list.

The messages move to the SBS Export folder.

8   Double-click the SBS Export folder.

The messages are now in the SBS Export folder.

Now that you have organized the messages that you need into a single folder, you can
create your export file.

Create an export file

1   From the File menu, choose Export Folder.

The Export Folders dialog box opens.

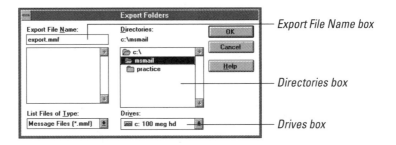

Export File Name box

Directories box

Drives box

2   In the Directories box, double-click the PRACTICE subdirectory in your
C:\MSMAIL directory.

Note   This stores the export file on your hard disk. If you want to put the file directly
on a floppy disk, you can specify a floppy disk drive in this dialog box.

---

3   In the Export File Name box, delete all of the text, and then type **expsbs**

Your export file will be named EXPSBS.MMF, as Microsoft Mail adds the MMF
extension for you.

4   Click OK.

A dialog box opens, asking if you want to create the file EXPSBS.MMF.

5   Click Yes.

After a few moments, the Export Folders dialog box opens.

Folders to Export box

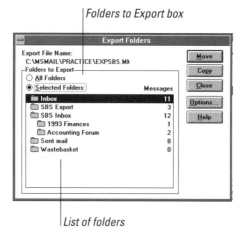

List of folders

6   Select the SBS Export folder.

Note   You can export multiple folders in one file. Simply select the folders you want
by clicking each while holding down CTRL, or choose All Folders instead of Selected
Folders, if you want to export all of your folders.

---

*Whenever you export
a folder, your
Personal Address
Book is also copied.*

7   Choose the Copy button.

The SBS Export folder and all of the messages in it are copied to your
EXPSBS.MMF file.

8   Choose the Close button.

The Export Folders dialog box closes.

The EXPSBS.MMF file is now on your hard disk, ready to be copied to a floppy disk
or another computer. You will see how to use this file in the next exercise, when you
import it.

Importing a Message File

When you arrive home or leave on your business trip and want to begin working on
your messages, you need to transfer your folder onto your home or portable computer.
To move the folder onto your home or portable computer, you import the folder with
the Import Folders command on the File menu. After you import the folder, you can
open the messages within the folder, reply to them or work on new messages, and save
the messages in the same folder when you are done. When you return to your office,
you can repeat the export/import process to bring the messages back to your work
computer, and send them through your Mail network.

Importing works like exporting, except that it copies folders from a message file into
your mailbox, rather than copying folders from your mailbox to a message file. In the
next exercise, you import the export file that you created earlier.

Import a message file

1   From the File menu, choose Import Folder.

The Import Folders dialog box opens.

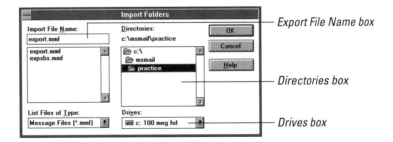

2   In the Directories box, double-click the PRACTICE subdirectory under the
C:\MSMAIL directory.

3   In the Import File Name list box, select EXPSBS.MMF.

This is the export file you created in the last exercise.

4   Click OK.

After a few moments, the Import Folders dialog box opens.

Folders to Import box

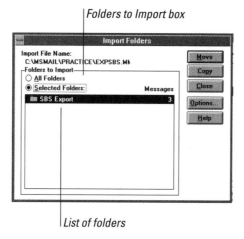

List of folders

5   Select the SBS Export folder, and then choose the Copy button.

A dialog box opens, warning you that a folder with a duplicate name exists. This occurs because you did not remove the original SBS Export folder when you created the export file.

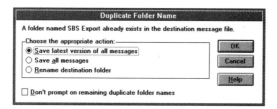

6   Select the "Rename destination folder" option, and then choose OK.

7   In the Rename Folder dialog box, type **SBS Export 1** and then choose OK.

The messages from the SBS Export folder from EXPSBS.MMF are copied into the SBS Export 1 folder in your mailbox.

8   Choose the Close button.

The Import Folders dialog box closes.

One Step Further

You can import and export all of the messages in a folder, or with the Options button in the Import or Export folder, you can specify only the files in a particular date range. Try importing only those messages sent on March 29, 1993.

1   From the File menu, choose Import Folder.

2   In the Import Folders dialog box, select the file IMPSBS.MMF under the C:\MSMAIL\PRACTICE directory.

3   Choose OK.

4   Select the SBS Import folder, and then choose the Options button.

The Options dialog box opens.

5   Choose the Messages Received or Modified option.

6   In the From text box, use the arrows to select the date 3/29/93.

7   In the To text box, use the arrows to select the date 3/29/93.

8   Choose OK, and then choose Copy.

Four messages that were last received or modified on 3/29/93 are copied to your mailbox in the folder SBS Import.

9   Choose Close.

If You Want to Continue to the Next Lesson

▶   Complete the Part 2 Review & Practice, or follow the instructions at the end of the Review & Practice to delete your practice folders.

▶   Minimize Microsoft Mail.

If You Want to Quit Mail for Now

▶   From the File menu, choose Exit And Sign Out.

Lesson Summary

To	Do this
Export a file	From the File menu, choose Export Folders. Choose the directory you want, then type the file name and choose OK. Select the folders you want, and then choose Copy. Choose Close.
Import a file	From the File menu, choose Import Folders. Choose the directory the file is in, select the file name, and then choose OK. Select the folders you want and choose Copy. Choose Close.

For online information about	From the Help menu, choose Contents and then
Exporting files	Choose "Managing Your Message File" and select the topic "Exporting Mail Folders."
Importing files	Choose "Managing Your Message File" and select the topic "Importing Mail Folders."

Preview of the Next Lesson

In the next lesson, you'll learn how to use Microsoft Schedule+ to organize your personal appointments. With Microsoft Schedule+, you will be able to create and edit various types of appointments and set reminders for them.

Review & Practice

In the lessons in Part 2, Working with Microsoft Mail for Windows, you learned skills to help you organize your messages, attach files and embed objects, set program defaults, and import and export message files. If you want to practice these skills and test your understanding before you proceed with the lessons in Part 3, you can work through the Review & Practice section following this lesson.

Part 2   Review & Practice

Before you move on to learning about Schedule+, practice the skills you learned in Part 2 by working through the steps in this Review & Practice section. You will sort your messages, create new folders, move messages into the folders, create a new message and attach a file, save the attachment, change your Mail Options, and create an export file of your new folders.

Scenario

You need to spend some time organizing your messages and setting your options. Also, you need to send your proposed budget in before the deadline. You decide to sort your messages by date received. Then you decide that you might be better off if you create some new folders to store some of the messages you will keep. You need to send your budget information, but you don't want to retype it, so you simply attach the file you were working on to the message. You also decide to change your options to a simpler setup and create an export file for your new folders so you can work at home.

You will review and practice how to:

- Sort messages.
- Create private folders.
- Move messages between folders.
- Attach a file to a message.
- Save an attached file.
- Set Mail options.
- Create an export file of saved messages.

Estimated practice time: 15 minutes

Step 1: Sort Messages

Open your SBS Inbox folder, and then sort your messages by date received with the most recent messages at the top. Use the menu or the column heading shortcut.

For more information on	See
Sorting messages	Lesson 3

Step 2: Create Folders and Move Messages

Create two new private, top-level folders called Marketing and Personal. Move any messages with the word "Marketing" in the subject from the SBS Inbox folder to the Marketing folder. Move the messages about "Lunch Meeting," "Suggestions," and "Parking Lot Resurfacing" from the SBS Inbox and Miscellaneous folders into the Personal folder.

For more information on	See
Creating folders	Lesson 3
Moving messages	Lesson 3

Step 3: Attach a File

Create a new message with the subject "Budget Figures" and the following text: "Here are the budget figures for next year." Attach the Microsoft Excel file BUDGET.XLS from your C:\MSMAIL\PRACTICE directory, and send the message to yourself.

For more information on	See
Attaching files	Lesson 4

Step 4: Save an Attached File

Open the message about budget figures and save the attached file to your hard drive in the C:\MSMAIL directory. (Remember, you do not need to have Microsoft Excel on your sytem to save the attached file.)

For more information on	See
Saving attached files	Lesson 4

Step 5: Set Mail Options

Change your options to have only the following options turned off: (1) Check spelling of messages before sending; (2) Sound chime when new messages arrive.

For more information on	See
Setting Mail options	Lesson 5

Step 6: Create an Export File

Create an export file that includes your new folders, Marketing and Personal. Name the file PRACEXP.MMF and place it in your C:\MSMAIL\PRACTICE directory.

For more information on	See
Creating an Export File	Lesson 6

If You Want to Continue to the Next Lesson

Delete practice folders and open Schedule+

1 In the folder list, select Marketing, Personal, Miscellaneous, and SBS Export, and then click the Delete button.

2 At the confirmation dialog box, choose OK.

3 Click the Minimize button on the Microsoft Mail for Windows program window.

4 Double-click the Schedule+ program icon.

If You Want to Quit Mail for Now

▶ From the File menu, choose Exit And Sign Out.

Working with Microsoft Schedule+

Working with Your Personal Schedule

Keeping track of all of the appointments you make can be difficult. Was the planning meeting on Thursday or Friday? Ten o'clock or twelve? In order to keep track of appointments, most people use a traditional appointment book, desk calendar, or daily planner. Microsoft Schedule+ can also keep track of your appointments, let you look up dates in a calendar, and show you a daily planner. Additionally, it can remind you of upcoming appointments and help you coordinate meetings with other people.

With Schedule+, you can see your appointments for the day in one view, look at your schedule for the next two weeks in another view, coordinate meetings, and check off your tasks in a task list organized by project. You can also have Schedule+ remind you in advance about each appointment and, if you like, print a copy of your schedule to carry with you or tack to your bulletin board.

In this lesson, you will learn how to use Schedule+ to create and organize different types of personal appointments with an electronic appointment book.

You will learn how to:

- Create and edit appointments.
- Set appointment reminders.
- Move and delete appointments.
- Create special types of appointments.
- Add daily notes.
- Print your schedule.

Estimated lesson time: 40 minutes

Start Mail and Schedule+

1   Double-click the Microsoft Mail icon.

For information about starting Microsoft Mail, see "Starting Microsoft Mail" in the "Getting Ready" section earlier in this book.

2   Type your name and password, and then press ENTER.

The Microsoft Mail window appears.

3   Click the Minimize button on the Microsoft Mail application window.

4   Double-click the Microsoft Schedule+ icon.

For information about starting Schedule+, see the "Getting Ready" section earlier in this book. The Schedule+ window appears, ready for you to create a new appointment.

5   Click the Maximize button on the Schedule+ application window.

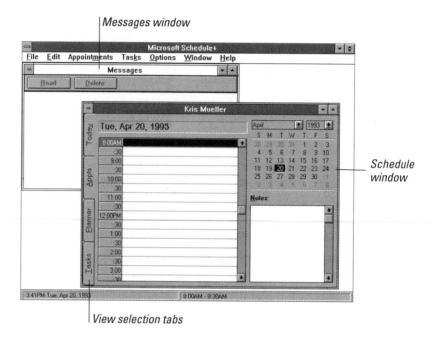

Creating Appointments

Suppose you have set a meeting for Friday morning from 10:00 to 12:00. You need to place it on your calendar or put a reminder somewhere so that you don't forget. Using Schedule+, you can easily add an appointment to your personal schedule.

You can create appointments by choosing the New Appointment command from the Appointments menu or by selecting the time directly on your Appointment Book. Either way, you can set the date and time, and add a description of the appointment.

In the next exercise, you will set up a two-hour appointment using Schedule+.

Note   To avoid confusion with any real appointments you might have in the near future, most of the exercises in this lesson have you set the year to 1999.

Use the New Appointment command to create an appointment

1 Click the Appts tab on the Schedule window.

This sets the view to your daily Appointment Book, if you had another view active.

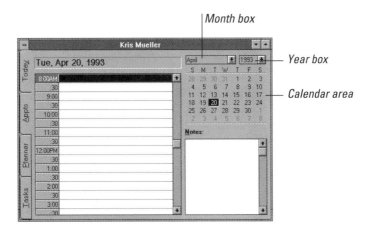

Month box

Year box

Calendar area

2 In the calendar area at the upper-right part of the Appointment Book, click the arrow next to the month box.

The month list box opens.

3 Select July.

4 Click the arrow next to the year box.

The year list box opens.

5 Scroll down, if necessary, and select 1999.

6 In the date calendar, click the 9th.

Your calendar shows Friday, July 9, 1999.

7   From the Appointments menu, choose New Appointment.

The Appointment dialog box opens.

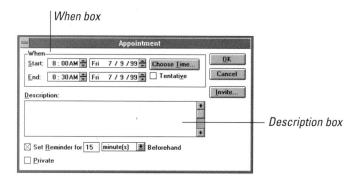

When box

Description box

8   In the When box, set the Start time to 10:00 A.M. and the End time to 12:00 P.M.

You can select the hour, minute, and A.M./ P.M. sections separately, and either use the selection arrows or type in the desired information.

Note   The selection arrows at the end of the box either increase or decrease the numbers in the box by certain increments. If you have selected the hour and clicked the up arrow, the hour will increase by one (2 to 3, for instance). If you select the minutes and then click the up arrow, the minutes will increase by 15-minute increments (10:00 to 10:15, for example).

---

9   Click in the Description box and type **Planning Committee**

10   Click OK.

The Appointment Book displays your new appointment.

You can also select the time and type a description directly in the Appointment Book itself to create a new appointment. In the next exercise, you create a new appointment without using the New Appointment dialog box.

Create an appointment by direct entry in the Appointment Book

1 In the time schedule of the Appointment Book, drag to select the time 1:00 P.M. to 2:00 P.M.

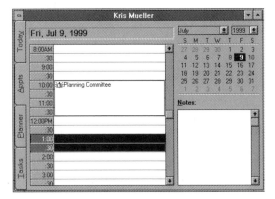

2 Type **Meet with Logo Committee**

Your second appointment of the day appears in the time schedule.

Setting Appointment Reminders

You can set an appointment reminder for any appointment that you create. A few minutes (or whatever period of time you specify) before an appointment, a dialog box will open listing the time and description of the appointment. Normally, appointment reminders are automatically set up for any new appointments you create. If you do not want to be reminded of a particular appointment, however, you can turn the reminder off either with the Appointment dialog box or with the Set Reminder command on the Appointments menu.

Note A 15-minute reminder is the default setting for Schedule+. In the One Step Further section at the end of this lesson, you can find out how to change general options such as this one.

Set and remove an appointment reminder

1 Double-click the Planning Committee appointment.

The Appointment dialog box opens.

2   Check to see if there is an X in the Set Reminder check box. If there is none, click
the box to place an X in it.

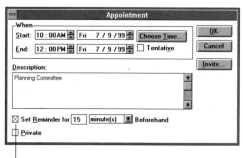

Set Reminder check box

3   In the minutes box, select the number and type **30**

4   Choose OK.

The Appointment dialog box closes. Notice that your appointment has a bell icon
in front of the description. This symbol tells you that there is a reminder set for
this appointment.

5   From the Appointments menu, choose Set Reminder.

The reminder for the appointment is removed. Notice that the bell icon in front of
the appointment description disappears.

Note   The Set Appointment Reminder command is a toggle switch. You can turn it
on or off by clicking the command. You can also use the shortcut CTRL+SHIFT+R to
turn appointment reminders on or off, or click the Set Reminders check box in the
Appointment dialog box.

Editing Appointments

If you need to change the description, time, or date of a meeting, you can easily alter the appointment in Schedule+. The quickest way to change an appointment description or time slot (within the same day) is to do so directly in the Appointment Book. To copy or delete an appointment, or to move it to a different day, you can use the appropriate commands on the Edit menu.

Suppose the nature of your Planning Committee appointment has been changed to include the entire company, and the time has been modified to one hour, starting at 10:30 A.M. In the next exercise, you will change both the time and the description of your Planning Committee appointment.

Edit an appointment's description and time

1   Select the Planning Committee appointment.

2   Drag to select the words "Planning Committee".

3   Type **Company Planning Meeting**

The description "Company Planning Meeting" replaces "Planning Committee".

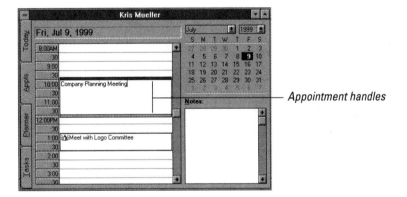

Appointment handles

Note   You can also change the description, time, or date of an appointment by using the Edit Appt command on the Edit menu. Or, you can double-click the appointment, and the Edit Appt dialog box will open, ready for you to make changes.

---

4   With the Company Planning Meeting appointment selected, point to the top appointment handle.

The pointer becomes a two-headed arrow. You can move appointments by dragging the top appointment handle to another time.

Note   You drag appointments to new times with the top appointment handle. You can also change the duration of an appointment by dragging the bottom appointment handle up or down.

---

5   Drag the top appointment handle down one slot to 10:30 A.M.

The appointment's start time changes to 10:30 A.M, and the end time changes to 12:30 P.M.

6   Drag the bottom appointment handle up two slots to 11:30 A.M.

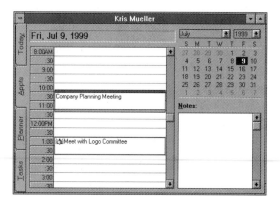

Copy an appointment

Suppose you learn that a second one-hour company planning meeting is scheduled for the following Thursday at 4:00 P.M. Instead of creating an entirely new appointment on that day, you can simply copy and paste from the existing appointment.

1   Select the Company Planning Meeting appointment.

2   From the Edit menu, choose Copy Appt.

3   In the Calendar, select Thursday, July 15, 1999.

4   In the Appointment Book, select the time 4:00 P.M.

5   From the Edit menu, choose Paste.

A copy of the Company Planning Meeting appointment is added to your schedule at 4:00 P.M. on Thursday, July 15, 1999.

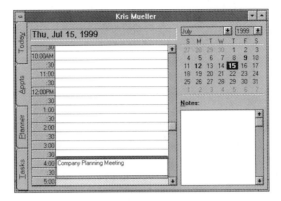

Move an appointment to a different day

Suppose you learn that the original Company Planning Meeting had to be postponed from Friday to the following Monday at 11:00 A.M. The Move Appt command allows you to move it quickly.

1   Switch the calendar to Friday, July 9, 1999, and then select the Company Planning Meeting at 10:30 A.M.

2   From the Edit menu, choose Move Appt.

The Move Appointment dialog box opens.

3   Use the arrows to change the date and time to Mon 7/12/99 at 11:00 A.M., and then click OK.

4   In the calendar, click the 9th, and then the 12th of July.

The Appointment Book shows that the Company Planning Meeting appointment is removed from Friday, July 9, and now appears on Monday, July 12, at 11:00 A.M.

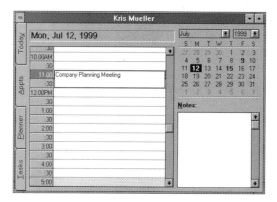

Delete an appointment

If an appointment is canceled, how do you remove it completely from the Appointment Book? You use the Delete Appt command on the Edit menu. In this exercise, you delete the Logo Committee meeting.

1   In the calendar, click Friday the 9th.

2   Select the Meet with Logo Committee appointment.

3   From the Edit menu, choose Delete Appt.

The appointment is deleted.

Note   If you delete an appointment accidentally, you can immediately restore it by choosing Undo Delete from the Edit menu.

Creating Special Types of Appointments

Suppose you sometimes have appointments that overlap, or you have a meeting every week at the same time, such as a department meeting. Rather than choosing between the overlapping meetings on your schedule, or entering every recurring meeting individually, you can create special types of appointments. You might also want to mark which appointments are not definite and which ones you want to keep hidden from others who have access to your calendar. With Schedule+, you can schedule *overlapping, recurring, tentative,* and *private* appointments.

Sorting Overlapping Appointments

If you have a 9:00 meeting that goes until 10:00, and another appointment from 9:45 to 10:30, for example, you can set these appointments as overlapping appointments on your schedule. If two appointments share part or all of the same time slot, they automatically appear as overlapping appointments. Both appointments will appear in your Appointment Book, splitting the space in the shared time slots.

Create an overlapping appointment

1 In your calendar, click Monday, July 12, 1999, and be sure that no appointments are selected.

2 From the Appointments menu, choose New Appointment.

Your new appointment will overlap with the Company Planning Meeting. The Appointment dialog box opens.

3 In the Start text box, use the arrows to select 10:15 A.M.

4 In the End box, use the arrows to select 11:15 A.M.

5 Click in the Description box, type **Department meeting** and then click OK.

The Appointment dialog box closes, and your appointment appears in the Appointment Book, overlapping with the Company Planning Meeting. Note that the start time is listed for any meeting that doesn't begin exactly on the hour or half-hour.

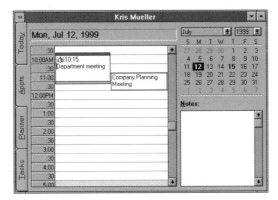

Setting Recurring Appointments

Suppose your Friday planning meeting happens every week. Rather than entering the same appointment over and over again for each week, you can set it as a recurring appointment.

To create a recurring appointment, you select the time and choose New Recurring Appt from the Appointments menu. You can enter information in the dialog box such as the appointment time, frequency, and description. In this exercise, you create a recurring appointment on the second Monday of each month.

Create a recurring appointment

1 Select the Company Planning Meeting appointment.

2 From the Appointments menu, choose New Recurring Appt.

The Recurring Appointment dialog box opens with the current appointment information filled in.

This Appointment Occurs box

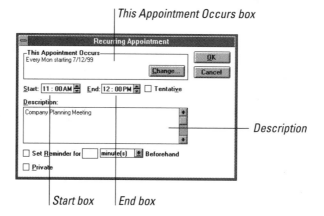

——— _Description_

Start box   _End box_

3   In the This Appointment Occurs box, click the Change button.

The Change Recurrence dialog box opens.

This Occurs box

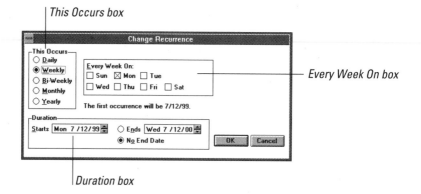

——— _Every Week On box_

Duration box

4   In the This Occurs box, select Monthly.

This makes the appointment recur every month.

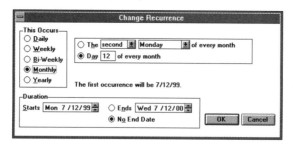

5   Select the option button next to "The second Monday of every month".

6   Click OK.

The Change Recurrence dialog box closes.

7   In the Recurring Appointment dialog box, click OK.

The Company Planning Meeting changes to a monthly recurring appointment. Notice the two circular arrows next to your new recurring appointment.

Note   Every recurring appointment has a small circular arrow icon in front of its description.

---

8   In the calendar, click the month box arrow and select August.

9   Select Monday, the 9th.

Your schedule shows August 9, 1999. Notice that your recurring Company Planning Meeting appointment is now on the schedule for next month as well as for every month after that.

Delete a recurring appointment

1   Select the Company Planning Meeting appointment.

2   From the Appointments menu, choose Edit Recurring Appts.

Note   You can use the Delete Appt command from the Edit menu to delete a *single* occurrence of a recurring appointment. To delete *every* instance of a recurring appointment, however, you must use the Edit Recurring Appts command from the Appointments menu.

3   With the Company Planning Meeting selected, choose the Delete button.

The recurring Company Planning Meeting appointment is deleted.

4   Choose the Close button.

5   In the calendar, click the month list and select July 12th.

Notice that the Company Planning Meeting appointment is gone from July 12, 1999.

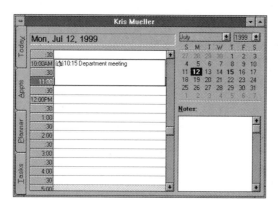

Suppose that you have an appointment that will recur every month during a limited period of five months. You can create a recurring appointment with a specific end date. In the next exercise, you will create a recurring appointment for every second Friday of the month from July to November.

Create another recurring appointment

1   In the calendar, click July 1st.

The Appointment Book shows July 1, 1999.

2   From the Appointments menu, choose New Recurring Appt.

The Recurring Appointment dialog box opens.

3   Set the Start time to 9:00 A.M. and the End time to 10:00 A.M.

4   Click in the Description box, and type **Marketing Planning Meeting**

5   In the This Appointment Occurs box, choose the Change button.

The Change Recurrence dialog box opens.

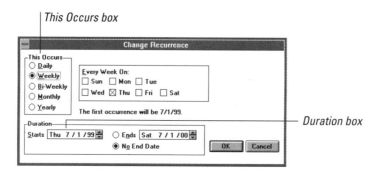

6   In the This Occurs box, select Monthly.

7   Select the option button next to "The first Thursday of every month".

8   Click the list boxes, and change "first" to "second", and "Thursday" to "Friday".

9   In the Duration box, use the arrows to change the Ends date to Tue 11/30/99.

10   Choose OK.

11   Choose OK again.

The New Recurring Appointment dialog box closes. Your new recurring appointment appears in your Appointment Book.

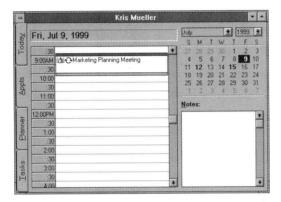

12   Using the calendar, look at appointments scheduled on the second Friday in each month from August through December, 1999.

The recurring appointment is scheduled through November, but does not appear in December, 1999.

Setting Tentative or Private Appointments

If you think that an appointment is likely to change or be canceled, you can enter it into your schedule as a tentative appointment. You can also mark your personal appointments as private.

As shown in Lesson 9, it is possible to view some of the appointments of other people on your Mail network. Perhaps you have a private appointment, like a medical appointment or a party, that you don't want others to see on your appointment book. You can mark appointments as private, which prevents others from viewing them. You can set an appointment as a tentative or private appointment in the Appointment dialog box when you first create it, or you can change it later with the Tentative or Private commands on the Appointments menu.

In the next exercise, you will create a new, private appointment, and then change it to a tentative one.

Create a private and a tentative appointment

1   In the calendar, select Monday, July 12, 1999.

2   On your schedule, select the time from 3:30 P.M. to 4:30 P.M.

3   From the Appointments menu, choose New Appointment.

The Appointment dialog box opens.

4   In the Description box, type **Doctor's appointment**

5   In the lower-left corner of the dialog box, click the Private check box.

Clicking the Private check box selects this option, making the appointment a private one.

6   Click OK.

Your new private appointment appears on your schedule. Notice the key symbol before the description "Doctor's appointment". This symbol indicates a private appointment.

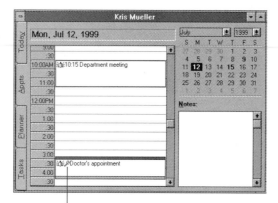

│*Key symbol designating a private appointment*

7   Be sure the new appointment is selected in the Appointment Book, and then from the Appointments menu, choose Tentative.

Notice that your new tentative appointment now has a gray shading, unlike regular appointments, which have a white background. The gray background tells you that the appointment is tentative.

Note   The Tentative command is a toggle switch. Choosing the Tentative command will turn that aspect of the appointment on or off. If it is currently tentative, with a check mark next to the command, choosing the Tentative command will turn it off (make it not tentative). If the appointment is currently not tentative, choosing Tentative will turn it on (make it tentative).

---

8   From the Appointments menu, choose Tentative.

Your appointment becomes permanent again.

Tip   There is a Private command on the Appointments menu as well. This command, like the Tentative command, is a toggle switch that changes your appointment to private if it is currently public, or public if it is currently private. There is also a Tentative check box in the Appointment dialog box.

Adding Daily Notes

Sometimes you'll have some extra information about an appointment that isn't part of the description but that you'd like to include in your schedule as a reminder. Perhaps you need to prepare a presentation for a meeting, or you need to check on someone's progress before meeting with someone else. With Schedule+, you can add notes to your Appointment Book. Simply move to the date you want in the Appointment Book and type the note in the Notes area. Notes are linked to the date on which they appear in the Appointment Book, but not to any specific appointment.

Add a note to the Appointment Book

1   Click in the Notes area.

2   Type **Finish budget before department meeting.**

The note appears in the Notes section of your Appointment Book for that day.

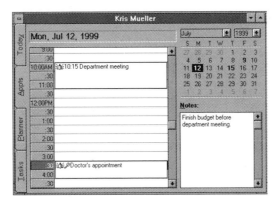

Printing Your Schedule

If you want to take your schedule with you when you leave the office, you have two choices. You can use Schedule+ on a portable computer that you take with you, or you can print your schedule in one of several formats. If you want to learn about using Schedule+ offline, refer to Appendix C at the end of this book. If you want to print your schedule, you simply need to decide what view you would like (weekly, daily, and so on), what date range you want to see, and what paper format (standard notebook, Junior size, and so on) you want to use. In the next exercise, you will print your schedule in weekly view, showing the week of July 4–July 10, on standard notebook-sized paper.

Print your schedule

1   From the File menu, choose Print.

The Print dialog box opens.

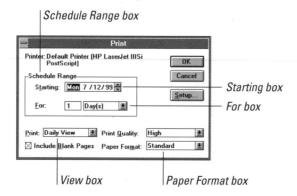

Schedule Range box

Starting box

For box

View box   *Paper Format box*

2   In the Print list box, select Weekly View.

3   Under Schedule Range, use the arrows to change the Starting date to Sun 7/4/99.

4   In the For box, select 2 Week(s).

Note   When you print your schedule in the Weekly View, it will print starting on the first day of the week. Usually, the first day of the week is set to Sunday, although you can change this setting with the General Options dialog box. You can learn more about the General Options dialog box in the One Step Further exercise at the end of this lesson.

---

5   In the Paper Format box, be sure that Standard is selected.

Your Print dialog box should look similar to the following illustration.

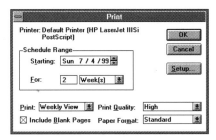

Note   If you are not currently hooked up to a printer, choose Cancel instead of OK in step 6.

6   Choose OK.

The Print dialog box closes. The Printing dialog box opens and shows your progress. The Printing dialog box closes when your print file has been sent to the printer.

One Step Further

Schedule+ has several default settings that control how the program functions or appears. With the General Options dialog box, you can control how your reminders will be set up, along with other options. Use the following steps to set your default reminders to 20 minutes before an appointment.

1   From the Options menu, choose General Options.

The General Options dialog box opens. With this dialog box, you can choose to automatically open Schedule+ offline, set reminder options, change the time your day starts and ends, change the day your week starts on, and set up other options for your schedule.

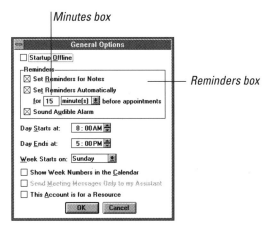

2   In the Reminders box, check to be sure that there is an X in the Set Reminders Automatically check box.

3   If there is an X, skip to step 4. If there is no X, click the box to add one.

4   In the Minutes text box, select the number and type 20.

This sets your automatic reminders for 20 minutes before each appointment.

5   Choose OK.

The General Options dialog box closes.

If You Want to Continue to the Next Lesson

Switch to the Task list

1   In the calendar, select Friday, July 9, 1999.

2   Click the Tasks tab on the Appointment Book.

If You Want to Quit Schedule+ for Now

▶   From the File menu, choose Exit And Sign Out.

Lesson Summary

To	Do this
Start Schedule+	Double-click the Microsoft Schedule+ icon. Type your name and password, and then click OK.
Create an appointment	In the Appointment Book, drag to select a time range and choose New Appointment from the Appointments menu. Fill in the description, and then click OK.
Edit an appointment	Select the appointment and choose Edit Appt from the Edit menu. To change only the time of the appointment, drag the top appointment handle to a new time on the day. To change only the duration, drag the bottom appointment handle to a different time. To change only the description, select the appointment, select the description text, and type the new description over it.
Create an overlapping appointment	Select the time and choose New Appointment from the Appointments menu. Type your description, and then click OK.
Create a recurring appointment	Choose New Recurring Appt from the Appointments menu. Fill in the description and time, and then click the Change button to change when the appointment occurs. Fill in the This Occurs, Every Week On, and Duration boxes, and then click OK. Click OK again.

To	Do this
Create a tentative appointment	Select the appointment and choose Tentative from the Appointments menu. Or, choose the Tentative option when creating the appointment.
Create a private appointment	Select the appointment and choose Private from the Appointments menu. Or, choose the Private option when creating the appointment.
Move an appointment on the same day	Drag the top appointment handle to another location on the date.
Move an appointment to a different day	Select the appointment and choose Move Appt from the Edit menu. Fill in the new date and time, and then choose OK.
Delete an appointment	Select the appointment. From the Edit menu, choose Delete Appt.
Set or remove an appointment reminder	Select the appointment and choose Set Reminder.
Add a note to a day	Click in the Notes box and type your note.
Print your schedule	From the File menu, choose Print. Select a date range, a view (Weekly, Daily, etc.), a paper format, and then choose OK.

For online information about	From the Help menu, choose Contents and then
Adding daily notes	Choose "Scheduling Your Appointments" and select the topic "Adding a Daily Note in the Appointment Book."
Creating appointments	Choose "Scheduling Your Appointments" and select the topic "Scheduling an Appointment."
Creating recurring appointments	Choose "Scheduling Your Appointments" and select the topic "Scheduling a Recurring Appointment."
Editing, moving, or deleting appointments	Choose "Scheduling Your Appointments" and select the topic "Changing or Deleting an Appointment."
Printing your schedule	Choose "Printing Your Schedule or Tasks" and select the topic "Printing Your Appointments and Daily Notes."
Setting appointment reminders	Choose "Scheduling Your Appointments" and select the topic "Setting Appointment Reminders."
Starting or Quitting Schedule+	Choose "Introduction to Microsoft Schedule+" and select the topic "Signing In to Schedule+" or "Quitting Schedule+."

For an online demonstration of	From the Help menu, choose Demos and then
Changing or deleting appointments	Click the title "Booking Appointments," and then choose the "Changing and Deleting Appointments" demonstration.
Creating appointments	Click the title "Booking Appointments," and then choose the "Scheduling Appointments" demonstration.
Creating recurring appointments	Click the title "Booking Appointments," and then choose the "Scheduling Recurring Appointments" demonstration.

For more information on	See the *Microsoft Schedule+ User's Guide*
Appointment reminders	Chapter 4, "Learning Schedule+"
Creating, editing, and deleting appointments	Chapter 4, "Learning Schedule+"
Making daily notes	Chapter 4, "Learning Schedule+"
Overlapping, private, recurring, and tentative appointments	Chapter 4, "Learning Schedule+"

Preview of the Next Lesson

In the next lesson, you'll learn how to use Schedule+ to generate a task list and view the tasks, set priorities for them, sort the tasks by various criteria, organize tasks by project, and add the tasks to your schedule with reminders.

Using the Task List

You've learned how to use Microsoft Schedule+ to organize your daily appointments, but what about all of the different tasks and projects that you work on each day? And how about all of those To Do lists cluttering your desk? You can use Schedule+ to generate and view a list of tasks, set priorities for them, sort the tasks by various criteria, and add the tasks to your schedule with reminders. You can also print your tasks in whatever order you like. In this lesson, you will learn to use Schedule+ to create a list of tasks and projects, set priorities and reminders, and add tasks to your Appointment Book schedule.

You will learn how to:

- Add tasks and projects to the Task list.
- Edit and delete tasks.
- Set task priorities.
- Sort tasks.
- Add tasks to your schedule.
- Set task reminders.

Estimated lesson time: 40 minutes

Start Mail and Schedule+

1   Double-click the Microsoft Mail icon.

For information about starting Microsoft Mail, see "Starting Microsoft Mail" in the "Getting Ready" section earlier in this book.

2   Type your name and password, and then press ENTER.

The Microsoft Mail window appears.

3   Click the Minimize button on the Microsoft Mail application window.

4   Double-click the Microsoft Schedule+ icon.

For information about starting Schedule+, see the "Getting Ready" section earlier in this book.

5   Click the Maximize button on the Schedule+ application window.

6   In the calendar, select Friday, July 9, 1999.

Adding Tasks and Projects to the Task List

Perhaps you have a department meeting coming up, and you need to make a presentation about your progress on a project. You might have several parts to the presentation and several different tasks for each part. Instead of listing them on paper and perhaps losing your list, you can use the *Task list* view in Schedule+ to record your tasks, set priorities, and set reminders for them.

You can create individual tasks in your Task list for anything you need to do. You can also set due dates and priorities for the individual tasks in your list. If you have a long list of tasks, or if you are involved with several different activities that each have their own tasks, you can create *projects* to organize the tasks. Projects are large categories under which you can have different individual tasks. For example, if you are organizing a day-long meeting or event, you will have many individual tasks that you need to perform such as scheduling a room, assigning presentations, calling a caterer, scheduling equipment, getting name tags, and so on. All of these tasks can be grouped under a project called "Organizing Company Meeting."

To create a new task, you use the New Task command from the Tasks menu or use the New Task box on the Task list. In the next exercise, you will create a new project for your department meeting and add tasks to it.

Create a new project and tasks

1 In the Schedule window, click the Tasks tab.

Alternatively, you can press ALT+T. The Task list appears.

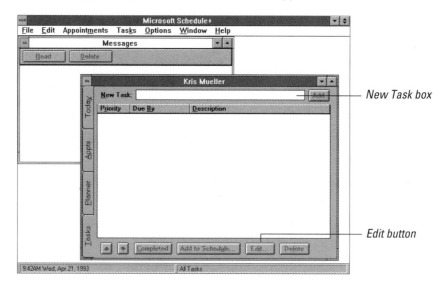

New Task box

Edit button

2   From the Tasks menu, choose New Project.

The New Project dialog box opens.

3   In the Name box, type **Coordinating Department Meeting** and then choose OK.

Your new project appears in the Task list.

4   Open the Tasks menu, and be sure the View By Project command is chosen.

The View By Project command is a toggle switch. If there is already a check mark by the command, simply close the menu. If there is no check mark, choose the command to activate it. View By Project allows you to see tasks listed under their respective projects.

New Task box

5   In the Task list, click to place your insertion point in the New Task box.

This text box lets you add a New Task by typing a description.

6   Type **Gather productivity data**

7   Choose the Add button, or press ENTER.

Your new task appears in the Task list.

8   Click in the New Task box, type **Finish presentation!** and then choose Add.

This task also appears in the Task list.

9   From the Tasks menu, choose New Task.

The New Task dialog box opens.

Due Date box

10   In the Description box, type **Call Chris about lunch**

11   In the Due Date box, select the By option button, and then use the arrows to select Mon 7/12/99.

This assigns a due date to your task.

12   Choose OK.

Your new task appears in the Task list with a due date.

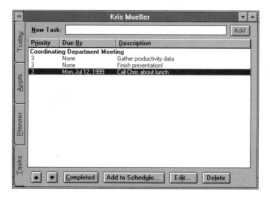

Editing Tasks

If the due date, priority, project, or even description of a task changes, you can edit the task to update the information. To edit a task, you select it in the Task list and then choose the Edit button. You can also use the Edit Task command on the Edit menu. If you need to change or remove a task's project designation, you can select the task and drag it to a different position in the list. In the next exercise, you will add a due date to your "Gather productivity data" task, and change the "Call Chris about lunch" task so that it is not related to any specific project.

Edit a task

1   Select the task "Gather productivity data", and then choose the Edit button.

The Task dialog box opens.

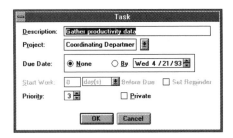

2   Click at the end of the description, press SPACEBAR, and add the phrase **for planning mtg**.

3   In the Due Date box, select By, and then use the arrows to select Fri 7/9/99.

4   Choose OK.

Your revised task is updated in the Task list.

5   In the Task list, select the task "Call Chris about lunch" and drag this task down below the last task name.

The "Call Chris about lunch" task moves to the top of the list, above any project name, so it is no longer part of a project.

6   Double-click the task "Call Chris about lunch".

The Task dialog box opens. Notice that the Project box has <None> selected.

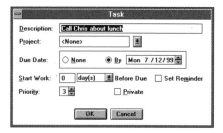

7 Choose Cancel.

The Task dialog box closes.

Setting Task Priorities

In your Task list, you might have some tasks that are more important than others. With Schedule+, you can assign different priorities for your tasks so you can easily decide which tasks need your attention first. You can assign each task a priority as either a single number (from 1 to 9) or a single letter (from A to Z). Numbered priorities take precedence over lettered priorities. For example, if you have a task with a priority of 4, and another with a priority of D, the task at priority 4 is a higher priority than the one at priority D. The default priority (the priority assigned if you do not specify a priority) is 3.

You can set the priority when you create a new task, or you can change it later using the Edit or Priority buttons on the Task list. The Priority buttons (up and down arrows at the lower-left corner of the Task list) let you increase or decrease the priority of a task without opening a dialog box or editing the task. If you want to change a task's priority by several levels, it might be easier to use the Edit button. In the next exercise, you will assign and change priorities for the tasks in your list using the Edit and Priority buttons.

Set a task priority

1 Select the "Gather productivity data..." task in the Task list.

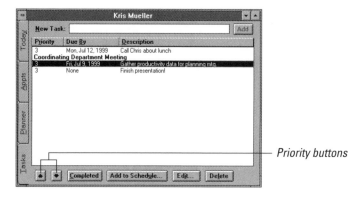

Priority buttons

2   Click the Up priority button.

The task priority changes to 2, a higher priority.

3   Select the "Call Chris about lunch" task, and then choose the Edit button.

4   In the Priority box, select the existing level (3), and then type **e**

5   Choose OK.

The task changes to the lower, lettered priority of E.

Sorting Tasks

If you want to see only active tasks (tasks with due dates that are current or past due), you can use the Show Active Tasks command on the Tasks menu. Past due tasks appear in red in the Task list.

What if you have a long list of tasks and you need to decide what to do first? Instead of looking through the whole list and guessing, you can sort the tasks by priority, by due date, by description, or by project. You can sort your tasks either from the Tasks menu or by using the Due By, Priority, and Description buttons at the top of the Task list.

Sort tasks

1   From the Tasks menu, choose View By Project.

This hides any project names so they don't appear in the Task list. The View By Project command is a toggle switch that you turned on earlier in this lesson. Choosing the command again now turns the view off.

2   From the Tasks menu, choose Sort By Priority.

Your tasks appear in order of priority, from highest to lowest.

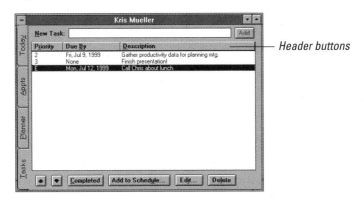

Header buttons

3   Click the Description header button at the top of the Task list.

Your tasks appear alphabetically by description.

Adding Tasks to Your Schedule

Perhaps you need to assign a specific time to work on a task. With the Add To Schedule button at the bottom of the Task list, you can add tasks to your schedule and specify a time and date to work on them. When you choose the Add To Schedule button, the Planner opens, allowing you to select the time block and date you want. When you add a task to your schedule, it remains on your Task list as well.

Add a task to your schedule and then remove it

1   Select the "Finish presentation!" task, and then choose the Add To Schedule button.

The Choose Time dialog box opens.

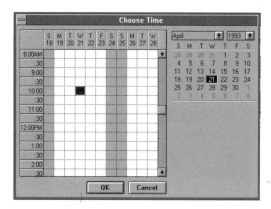

2   In the calendar, select July 15, 1999.

3   Drag to select the time 1 to 3 P.M. on Thursday, July 15, 1999, and then choose OK.

The task is added to your schedule.

4   Click the Appts tab on the Schedule window.

5 In the calendar, be sure that July 15, 1999 is selected.

Notice your "Finish presentation!" task is now an appointment from 1 to 3 P.M. The project name also appears in parentheses.

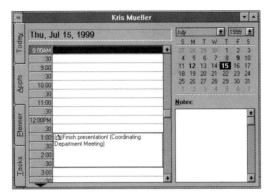

6 Select the "Finish presentation!" appointment.

7 From the Edit menu, choose Delete Appt.

Your "Finish presentation!" appointment is deleted.

8 Click the Tasks tab on the Schedule window.

Notice that your "Finish presentation!" task remains in the Task list, even though it was added to and deleted from your Appointment Book.

Setting Task Reminders

Sometimes, on a particularly time-sensitive task, you need a reminder to be sure you complete it on time. You can set reminders for tasks, just as you can for appointments, with either the Edit button or the Edit Task command. In order to set a reminder, you must assign a due date to the task. In this exercise, you will set a task reminder for your "Gather productivity data..." task.

Note If your default setting in the General Options dialog box is set to automatically add reminders to your appointments, then when you add a task to your schedule, you automatically set a reminder for that task. If you look for that task in the Appointment Book, you will see a bell symbol that tells you a reminder is set.

Set a task reminder

1 Select the "Gather productivity data..." task, and then choose the Edit button.

The Task dialog box opens.

2   In the Due Date box, choose the By option button.

3   Click the up arrow on the By text box three times.

This sets the due date at three days from Friday, or the following Monday.

4   Click the Set Reminder check box, and then choose OK.

Choosing OK sets the reminder and closes the Task dialog box. Notice that the same bell symbol used in the Appointment Book appears in your Task list in front of the task with a reminder.

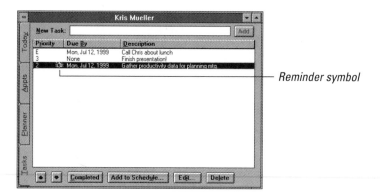

—— *Reminder symbol*

Deleting Tasks

If you've completed a task, you can delete the task from your Task list. There are several ways to delete a task. You can choose Delete Task from the Edit menu if you only need to delete a task. If you have completed a task and would like to keep a record of it, you can click the Completed button on the Task list. You can also delete entire projects from your Task list with the Delete Task command.

Note   Before you delete any tasks, you might want to print a copy of the list for future reference. Just as you can print your appointments, you can print your Task list in order to have a reference copy. You simply sort the tasks in whatever order you prefer, choose the Print command from the File menu, and pick a paper format. When you are in the Task list view, the Print command is automatically set to print your tasks unless you select another item in the Print list box.

When you use the Delete Task command, the task is removed from the Task list and no record of it remains. When you mark a task as completed, it is removed from the Task list and placed in the Notes section of your Appointment Book for the current day. In the next exercises, you will mark one task as completed, and then delete your other tasks and projects from your Task list.

Mark a task as completed

1 In your Task list, select the "Gather productivity data..." task.

2 Click the Completed button at the bottom of the Task list.

The "Gather productivity data..." task is removed from the Task list.

3 Click the Today tab on the Schedule window.

The Schedule window displays the current day's Appointment Book. Notice the text that begins with "Done". This is your completed task.

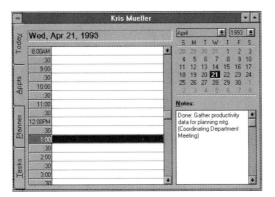

4 Select the text about this task in the Notes area, and then press DEL.

The note is deleted.

5 Click the Tasks tab on the Schedule window.

The Schedule window displays the Task list.

Delete tasks

1 From the Tasks menu, choose View by Project.

2 Select the "Coordinating Department Meeting" project, and then choose the Delete button.

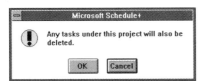

3 Choose OK to delete any tasks under the project.

The "Coordinating Department Meeting" project is removed from the Task list.

4   Select the "Call Chris about lunch" task, and then choose the Delete button.

The "Call Chris about lunch" task is deleted.

One Step Further

Just as you can create private and recurring appointments, you can create private and recurring tasks. In the previous lesson, you created a recurring appointment for a planning meeting. With the Task list, you can set up recurring tasks for that meeting. In this exercise, you create a new project for your planning meeting and add a new recurring task for the project.

If you need to delete all occurrences of a recurring task, you can use the Edit Recurring Tasks command on the Tasks menu, and then delete the recurring task. If you use the Delete Task command in the Task list to delete a recurring task, you will delete only the selected occurrence. When you use the Edit Recurring Tasks command, you can delete every occurrence of the recurring task.

Try creating a recurring task, and then deleting every occurrence of the task.

Create recurring tasks

1   From the Tasks menu, choose New Recurring Task.

The Recurring Task dialog box opens.

2   In the Description box, type **Remind department** and then choose the Change button.

The Change Recurrence dialog box opens.

This Occurs box

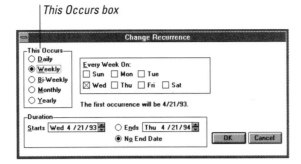

3   In the This Occurs box, select Monthly.

4   Select Last, and then Friday.

The last Friday of every month is selected.

5   In the Starts box, select the year and type 99.

6   Choose OK.

The Change Recurrence dialog box closes.

7   Choose OK again.

The New Recurring Task dialog box closes and your task appears in your Task list. Notice the Recurring Task symbol next to the description.

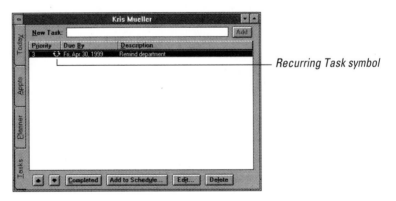

Recurring Task symbol

Delete a recurring task

1   Select the "Remind department" task.

2   From the Tasks menu, choose Edit Recurring Tasks.

The Edit Recurring Tasks dialog box opens.

Delete button

3   In the Edit Recurring Tasks dialog box, select "Remind department" and then choose the Delete button.

The recurring task is deleted.

4   Choose Close.

The Edit Recurring Tasks dialog box closes.

If You Want to Continue to the Next Lesson

Switch to the Appointment Book

1   Choose the Appt tab on the Appointment Book.

2   In the calendar, switch to Friday, July 9, 1999.

If You Want to Quit Schedule+ for Now

▶   From the File menu, choose Exit And Sign Out.

Lesson Summary

To	Do this
Create a task	Type in the New Task box and choose Add. Or, choose New Task from the Tasks menu, fill in the description, project, due date, and priority, and then choose OK.
Edit a task	Select the task and choose the Edit button. Make your changes, and then choose OK.
Set a task priority	Select the task and choose the Edit button, change the priority, and then choose OK. Or, select the task and click the up or down arrow button at the bottom of the Task list.

To	Do this
Sort tasks	From the Tasks menu, choose Sort by Priority, Sort by Due Date, Sort by Description, or View by Project. Or, click the Priority, Due by, or Description header button.
Add a task to your schedule	Select the task and choose the Add to Schedule button. Select a time and choose OK.
Set a task reminder	Select the task and choose the Edit button. Click the Set Reminder check box and choose OK.
Print your tasks	In the Task list, sort your tasks by Project, Due Date, Priority, or Description. From the File menu, choose Print. Select a Paper Format, and then choose OK.
Delete your tasks	In the Task list, select the task or project that you want to delete, and then choose the Delete button.
Mark a task as completed	In the Task list, select the task, and then choose the Completed button.

For online information about	From the Help menu, choose Contents and then
Adding tasks to your schedule	Choose "Working With Your Task List" and select the topic "Adding a Task to Your Appointment Book."
Creating tasks and projects	Choose "Working With Your Task List" and select the topic "Adding a Project" or "Adding a Task."
Editing or deleting tasks	Choose "Working With Your Task List" and select the topic "Changing or Deleting a Task or Project."
Printing tasks	Choose "Printing Your Schedule or Tasks" and select the topic "Printing Your Tasks."
Setting task priorities	Choose "Working With Your Task List" and select the topic "Changing a Task's Priority."
Setting task reminders	Choose "Working With Your Task List" and select the topic "Setting Task Reminders."
Sorting tasks	Choose "Working With Your Task List" and select the topic "Sorting and Displaying Your Projects and Tasks."

For an online demonstration of	From the Help menu, choose Demos and then
Adding and changing tasks	Click the title "Working with Your Task List," and then choose the "Adding and Changing Tasks" demonstration.
Organizing your Task list	Click the title "Working with Your Task List," and then choose the "Organizing Your Task List" demonstration.

For more information on	See the *Microsoft Schedule+ User's Guide*
Using the Task list	Chapter 4, "Learning Schedule+"

Preview of the Next Lesson

In the next lesson, you'll learn how to view your schedule and those of other people with the Planner. You'll also learn to send meeting requests, receive responses, and reschedule meetings.

Using the Planner to Schedule Meetings

Note   Because this lesson explores the interactive aspects of Schedule+, you need to recruit some help from one or two other people on your network in order to complete the exercises. Find at least one person on your network who will give you access to personal schedules and cooperate with your practice meeting requests.

As you learned in the previous two lessons, the Appointment Book and Task list can help you get your own schedule and tasks under control. But you still might find it difficult to coordinate meetings with the other people in your office. Using Schedule+ can help with this problem, too. With Schedule+, you can use the Planner to view your schedule and those of others on your network, and to schedule meetings at mutually available times. You can even send out meeting requests and receive the responses with Schedule+. You can also change meetings and inform the attendees of the changes with Schedule+.

In this lesson, you will learn how to use the Planner view and the Messages window in Schedule+ to view open times in your schedule and in other people's schedules, and to plan and confirm meetings at mutually convenient times.

You will learn how to:

- View your schedule with the Planner.
- View other people's schedules.
- Request meetings.
- View responses to meeting requests.
- Change meeting times.

Estimated lesson time: 40 minutes

Start Mail and Schedule+

1   Double-click the Microsoft Mail icon.

For information about starting Microsoft Mail, see "Starting Microsoft Mail" in the "Getting Ready" section earlier in this book.

2   Type your name and password, and then press ENTER.

The Microsoft Mail window appears.

3   Click the Minimize button on the Microsoft Mail application window.

4   Double-click the Microsoft Schedule+ icon.

For information about starting Schedule+, see the "Getting Ready" section earlier in this book.

5   Click the Maximize button on the Schedule+ application window.

6   Find one or two people on your network who will give you access to their schedules and who will respond to your practice meeting requests.

7   In your Schedule window, click the Appts tab, and then use the calendar to switch to Friday, July 9, 1999.

Your Appointment Book displays the date "Fri, Jul 9, 1999."

View Your Own Schedule with the Planner

With the Appointment Book view, you can see all of your appointments for the day in some detail. With the Task list, you can see all of your tasks. But what if you want a longer range view of your time commitments, perhaps by the week? The Schedule window has a view called the *Planner* that lets you see one to two weeks of scheduled time on a page, depending on what size your window is. With the Planner, you can easily see the times that are blocked–off on your schedule for existing appointments, and which times are available for new meetings or appointments.

Note   You can view any period of time in the past or future by using the calendar to switch to another week's view.

If you've forgotten what a particular appointment is for, or if you need more details about an appointment, you can double-click the blocked off time period to open the Appointment Book and take a closer look. In the next exercise, you will open the Planner view and look over your full schedule. Then you will check specific details for an appointment.

View your own schedule

1   Choose the Planner tab.

The Planner opens. Notice that the times when you have an appointment or meeting are marked, but no details are shown.

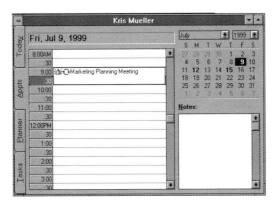

To see as many days as you need in the Planner, you can either maximize the window, or enlarge it by dragging the borders.

Calendar

Change
Attendees button

Scheduled appointment

2   Double-click the bar representing an appointment on Friday, July 9.

The window switches to the Appointment Book view, showing the description of the appointment and any symbols for reminders or recurring appointments.

3   Click the Today tab on the Appointment Book.

The Appointment Book shows the appointments for the current day.

Viewing Other People's Schedules

In the Planner view, you can see at a glance when your schedule is open for new appointments. But how can you find out when other people are available so you can set the time and date for a meeting? With Schedule+ and your network, you can view other people's schedules when you need to determine the best time for a meeting.

When you want to plan a meeting, you can open the Planner, change the list of attendees to reflect the people you want to invite, and locate an open time in everyone's schedules.

Note You can specify who can access your appointment book and how much they can do with it. Using Set Access Privileges on the Options menu, you can decide which people on your network are given any of the following privileges: view your free/busy times, view your appointments and tasks, create appointments and tasks on your schedule, and modify appointments and tasks on your schedule. The default is to view your free/busy times only.

In the next exercise, you coordinate meeting schedules with the one or two other network users that you recruited. You will select them as attendees and view their schedules in the Planner. This lesson will be the most useful and interesting if you and your coworkers have appointments scheduled. If you don't have any on the current page, you can add some, or move to a date in the future when you all have appointments.

View other people's appointments

1   Click the Planner tab on the Schedule window.

2   Choose the Change button on the right side of the window, near the list of attendees.

    The Select Attendees dialog box opens. It looks like the Address Book in Microsoft Mail.

3   Hold down CTRL and select the names in the list of those cooperating with you on this lesson.

Holding CTRL lets you select multiple, non-contiguous items in a list.

4   Choose the Add button, and then choose OK.

The names appear in the Attendees list, and the times they have scheduled appear on the Planner in a different color from your own appointments.

Note   Your schedule appears in blue and other people's schedules appear in gray unless you changed your colors with the Display command on the Options menu.

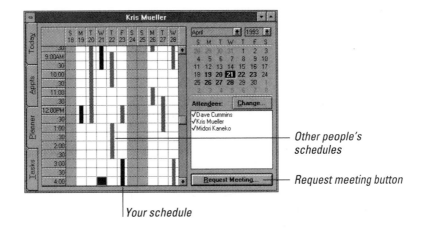

Other people's schedules

Request meeting button

Your schedule

Tip   You can show or hide other people's schedule information by clicking their names in the Attendees box. Clicking a name in the Attendees box turns that person's information on or off. A check mark in front of a name indicates that that person's information is showing in the Planner. An X in front of a name means that the selected time block overlaps an appointment in that person's schedule. If there is no check mark or X, that person's schedule does not appear.

Scheduling Meetings

Now that you can view other people's schedules as well as your own, you can determine the best time to have a meeting and communicate the meeting plan to the others involved. Although you could switch to Microsoft Mail and send out messages inviting people to the meeting, Schedule+ provides a better way. You simply select the time and choose the Request Meeting button. A Send Request form (similar to the Send Note form in Microsoft Mail) opens with the attendees' names, and the meeting time filled in. You can send this message directly from Schedule+. In the next exercise, you select a time in the Planner and send a meeting request to the other people who will be attending.

Schedule and request a meeting

1 Drag to select an empty time block, two hours long, in the current week.

This selects a time for your meeting.

Tip When you have several people to invite to a meeting and can't immediately see a time when they are all available, you can use the Auto–Pick feature to find the first available time. You use Auto–Pick to find a time that is open in all schedules. To use Auto–Pick, switch to the Planner view, select your attendees, and then choose the Auto–Pick command from the Appointments menu.

---

2 Choose the Request Meeting button.

A Send Request form opens with the time and the attendee names filled in.

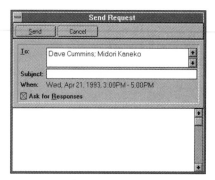

3 In the Subject box, type **Project Meeting**

Note You can also type any additional information you want in the message area.

---

4 Make sure there is a check mark in the Ask For Responses check box, and then choose the Send button.

Choosing Send sends your meeting request to the people in the To box. When you request a meeting, the meeting automatically appears in your Appointment Book.

5 Choose OK in the dialog box notifying you that the meeting has been booked.

Note The appointment will be added to the invitees' schedules after they have accepted or tentatively accepted your invitation.

---

6 Be sure to ask your volunteers to send responses to your request so you can complete the exercises later in this lesson.

Viewing Responses to Meeting Requests

You can also read meeting requests and responses in Microsoft Mail. Meeting requests and responses appear in both your Schedule+ Messages window and your Mail Inbox.

When you send out meeting requests, you can view the responses from other attendees without leaving Schedule+. The Messages window displays either responses to your requests or any requests from someone else. From the Messages window, you can read a message by double-clicking the message to open it. When you minimize the Message window, its icon looks similar to your Inbox and Outbox in Microsoft Mail.

When you send a meeting request, the invitees can respond in three ways: Accept, Decline, and Tentative. When they receive a meeting request, they respond with one of these options and send a message back to you indicating whether they will attend or not.

If they choose the Attend button, the meeting is added to their schedule, and their message to you appears with a check mark. If they decline, the meeting is not scheduled, and their message appears with an X. If they are not sure whether they can come and choose the Tentative button, the meeting is scheduled but marked as tentative, and their message appears with a question mark.

Open the Messages window and read a response

1 From the Window menu, choose Messages.

The Message window opens. Notice that the response messages have a check, an X, or a question mark in front of the name of the person responding. These marks help you see at a glance who has accepted or declined your request for a meeting. Meeting requests that you receive from others do not have any marks in front of the description.

Note If you don't have any messages yet, wait for a moment, or check with your volunteers to be sure that they responded.

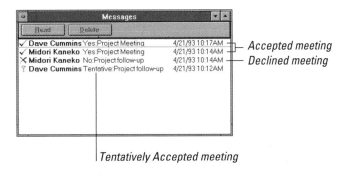

2   Double-click the first message in the list to open it.

3   Double-click the Control-menu box on the message.

The message closes. Notice that unread messages appear in bold, while read messages are in plain text.

Changing Meetings

Sometimes you will find that, although the schedules looked clear for the meeting time when you viewed them in your Planner, something might come up later, or people you invited might have other unlisted appointments. When someone declines a meeting, or asks if you could reschedule it, you can do so without difficulty.

To reschedule a meeting, you simply move the appointment to its new time in your Appointment Book as demonstrated in Lesson 7. A dialog box will then open, asking if you want to notify the other attendees of the change. When you choose OK, a new Meeting request will open that you can fill in as before.

Change a meeting time

1   Switch to the Schedule window, and double-click the time slot you chose for the Project Meeting.

The Appointment Book opens to the date of the meeting.

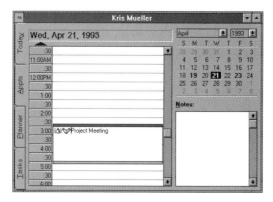

2   Select the Project Meeting appointment.

3   Use the top appointment handle to drag the appointment to a position two hours later.

A dialog box opens, asking if you want to notify the other attendees of the change in meeting times.

4 Choose Yes.

5 In the message area, type **Sorry, change in schedule!** and choose the Send button.

One Step Further

Sometimes you might need to find out more information than simply when someone else is busy. To view details about other people's appointments, you can view their Appointment Books. Before you try to view other people's Appointment Books, however, you need to be sure that they have given you access to read appointments and tasks.

Note To change the access privileges in Schedule+, choose Set Access Privileges from the Options menu. Select a name and set the access privileges, or set your default access privileges.

---

1 From the File menu, choose Open Other's Appt Book.

2 Scroll through the list and select the name of one of your volunteers.

If the list is long, type the first few letters of the name.

3 Choose Add, and then choose OK.

If you have access to the person's schedule, the Appointment Book opens. If you get an error message, have the person choose Set Access Privileges from the Options menu and check your name in the dialog box.

Note When you view other people's Appointment Books, you can see all of their appointments except appointments marked as Private. The Task list also shows all tasks except those marked as Private.

---

4 Choose the Tasks tab to view the person's tasks.

5 Choose the Today tab to view the person's appointments for today.

6 Double-click the Control-menu box on the other person's Appointment Book.

The Appointment Book closes.

If You Want to Quit Schedule+

▶ From the File menu, choose Exit And Sign Out.

To delete the practice appointments you created in this part, refer to the steps at the end of the Part 3 Review & Practice.

Lesson Summary

To	Do this
View your schedule	Choose the Planner tab in the Schedule window.
View other schedules	In the Planner, choose the Change button by the list of Attendees. Select the names you want, choose Add, and then choose OK.
Request meetings	Select a time, choose the Request Meeting button, fill in the subject and any comments, and then choose the Send button.
View messages	Choose the Messages window from the Window menu, or double-click the minimized Messages window.
Receive responses	Open the Messages window, select the response, and choose Read.
Change meetings and notify attendees	Select the appointment in your Appointment Book. Drag the top appointment handle to another position. Choose OK to send a notice of the change in time. Choose the Send button to send the message.

For online information about	From the Help menu, choose Contents and then
Changing meetings	Choose "Setting Up and Managing Meetings" and select the topic "Rescheduling or Canceling a Meeting."
Requesting meetings	Choose "Setting Up and Managing Meetings" and select the topic "Setting Up a Meeting."
Viewing messages	Choose "Setting Up and Managing Meetings" and select the topic "Responding to a Meeting Request."
Viewing other people's schedules	Choose "Viewing or Updating Another User's Schedule" and select the topic "Viewing Another User's Appointment Book or Task List."

For an online demonstration of	From the Help menu, choose Demos and then
Changing meetings	Click the title "Scheduling Meetings," and then choose the "Managing Meetings" demonstration.
Requesting meetings	Click the title "Scheduling Meetings," and then choose the "Setting Up Meetings" demonstration.
Viewing messages	Click the title "Scheduling Meetings," and then choose the "Responding to Meeting Requests" demonstration.

For more information on	See the *Microsoft Schedule+ User's Guide*
Requesting or changing meetings	Chapter 4, "Learning Schedule+"
Using the Planner	Chapter 4, "Learning Schedule+"
Viewing messages	Chapter 4, "Learning Schedule+"

Review & Practice

In the lessons in Part 3, Working with Schedule+, you learned skills to help you organize your personal schedule, create task lists, and schedule meetings with other people on your network. If you want to practice these skills and test your understanding, you can work through the Review and Practice section following this lesson. Pay special attention to the steps for deleting practice appointments at the end of the Review & Practice.

Part 3   Review & Practice

Before moving on to planning your own schedule, practice the skills you learned in Part 3 by working through the steps in this Review & Practice section. You will create a new recurring appointment, edit the reminder time, create a new task in the Task list, check your schedule and those of other people, and request a meeting.

Scenario

You need to set up a monthly meeting with the Accounting group. You begin by setting up a monthly appointment for yourself, and then changing the reminder for the week before. Next, you create a task in the Task list to organize the meeting and set the agenda. Once you've taken care of your tasks, you check your schedule and the schedules of the other Accounting people, and request a meeting. When the responses arrive, you check the Message window to see if everyone can make the meeting.

You will review and practice how to:

- Create and edit special types of appointments.
- Move and delete appointments.
- Create and edit tasks in the Task list.
- View your schedule with the Planner.
- View other people's schedules.
- Request meetings.
- View messages.

Estimated practice time: 15 minutes

Step 1:   Create and Edit a Recurring Appointment

Create a new recurring appointment with the description "Accounting Meeting" for the last Thursday of every month. Change the appointment's reminder to remind you one week before the event.

For more information on	See
Creating and editing appointments	Lesson 7

Step 2:   Move and Delete an Appointment

Move the appointment to the last Wednesday of the month, and change the time to 9:30 A.M. Then delete the appointment.

For more information on	See
Moving and deleting appointments	Lesson 7
Creating special types of appointments	Lesson 7

Step 3:   Create and Edit Tasks in the Task List

Switch to the Task list and create a new project called Accounting meeting. Create a new task called Set Agenda. Change the Set Agenda due date to the last Monday of the month.

For more information on	See
Creating and editing projects and tasks	Lesson 8

Step 4:   View Your Schedule and Other Schedules with the Planner

Switch to your Planner and check the last Wednesday of the month. Open another person's Appointment Book and check that person's schedule for that day.

For more information on	See
Viewing your schedule	Lesson 9
Viewing other schedules	Lesson 9

Step 5:   Request Meetings and View Messages

Request an accounting meeting for 9:30 to 10:30 A.M. on the last Wednesday of the month. Open the Messages window to see the responses.

For more information on	See
Requesting meetings	Lesson 9
Viewing messages	Lesson 9

Delete Appointments and Exit Schedule+

Follow these steps to delete the practice appointments you created in the lessons of Part 3, and then quit Schedule+.

1 In the Calendar, select Friday, July 9, 1999.

2 From the Appointments menu, choose Edit Recurring Appts.

3 In the list of recurring appointments, select "Marketing Planning Meeting" and choose the Delete button.

4 Choose the Close button.

5 In the Appointment Book, switch to Monday, July 12, 1999, and then select the "Doctor's Appointment" appointment and choose Delete Appt from the Edit menu.

6 In the Appointment Book, select the text in the Note box, and then press DEL.

7 Select the "Department Meeting" appointment and then press DEL.

8 In the Appointment Book, switch to Friday, July 15, 1999, select the "Company Planning Meeting" appointment, and then press DEL.

9 Switch to the Messages window, select each message, and choose the Delete button.

10 From the File menu, choose Exit And Sign Out.

Appendixes

Keyboard Equivalents

The following tables of shortcut and access keys can help you perform actions and commands in Microsoft Mail for Windows and Microsoft Schedule+ without using a mouse. *Shortcut keys* are substitutes for menu commands. Instead of opening the menu and then choosing a command, the shortcut key or key combination (such as CTRL+*letter*) carries out the command directly. *Access key* sequences (usually ALT, *letter, letter*) open the menu and then choose the command, producing the same sequence of actions that you can perform with the mouse.

Access keys can often be faster than reaching for the mouse if you are more comfortable with the keyboard. And, access keys are always indicated on the menus and commands themselves by underlined letters. Shortcut keys can be even quicker because they bypass the menus altogether, but you have to memorize them. Many shortcut key combinations are listed in the menus next to the corresponding commands. A few shortcuts, however—such as those for Cut, Copy and Paste—can be used with most Windows applications, and can save you a lot of time in the long run.

Keys and Commands for Microsoft Mail for Windows

The following tables list commands or actions in Microsoft Mail for Windows and their corresponding shortcut or access key combinations.

Microsoft Mail Shortcut Keys

To	Press
Change folder properties	ALT+ENTER
Check Spelling	F7
Compose a new message	CTRL+N
Copy	CTRL+C
Cut	CTRL+X
Delete	CTRL+D or DEL
Forward a message	CTRL+F
Move a message	CTRL+M
Open Help (context-sensitive)	F1
Open the Inbox	CTRL+G
Paste	CTRL+V

To	Press
Print	CTRL+P
Reply to a message	CTRL+R
Reply to all addressees	CTRL+A
Turn the toolbar on or off	CTRL+T
Undo	CTRL+Z

Microsoft Mail Access Keys

To	Press
Arrange icons	ALT, W, A
Cascade windows	ALT, W, C
Change folder properties	ALT, F, F
Change the password	ALT, M, C
Compose a new message	ALT, M, N
Copy a message or folder	ALT, F, C
Copy selection to the Clipboard	ALT, E, C
Create a new folder	ALT, F, N
Cut selection to the Clipboard	ALT, E, T
Delete a message or folder	ALT, F, D
Delete selection	ALT, E, D
Edit embedded object	ALT, E, O
Exit and sign out	ALT, F, T
Exit without signing out	ALT, F, X
Export a folder or folders	ALT, F, E
Find a message	ALT, F, G
Forward a message	ALT, M, F
Get information about Microsoft Mail for Windows	ALT, H, A
Import a message file	ALT, F, I
Insert an object	ALT, E, I
Insert an object from a file	ALT, E, F

To	Press
Make a backup	ALT, M, B
Move a message or folder	ALT, F, M
Open a message or folder	ALT, F, O
Open a new window	ALT, W, N
Open Help Contents	ALT, H, C
Open Help Index	ALT, H, I
Open the Address Book	ALT, M, D
Open the Inbox	ALT, V, I
Open the list of Personal Groups	ALT, M, G
Open the Message Finder	ALT, F, G
Paste Clipboard information	ALT, E, P
Paste with special formatting	ALT, E, S
Print a message	ALT, F, P
Reply to a message	ALT, M, R
Reply to all addressees of a message	ALT, M, A
Save a message as a text file	ALT, F, S
Save an attached file	ALT, F, A
Select everything	ALT, E, A
Set options	ALT, M, O
Set up the printer	ALT, F, R
Show/Hide status bar	ALT, V, B
Show/Hide toolbar	ALT, V, T
Sort messages by date	ALT, V, D
Sort messages by priority	ALT, V, Y
Sort messages by sender	ALT, V, S
Sort messages by subject	ALT, V, J
Split windows	ALT, V, P
Start online Demos	ALT, H, D
Tile windows	ALT, W, T

To	Press
Undo the last action	ALT, E, U
View new messages	ALT, V, N
View shared or private folders	ALT, V, F

Keys and Commands for Microsoft Schedule+

The following tables list commands or actions in Microsoft Schedule+ and their corresponding shortcut or access key combinations.

Microsoft Schedule+ Shortcut Keys

To	Press
Automatically pick a meeting time	CTRL+A
Copy	CTRL+C
Copy an appointment	CTRL+Y
Create a new appointment	CTRL+N
Create a new recurring appointment	CTRL+R
Create a new task	CTRL+T
Create a private appointment	CTRL+SHIFT+P
Create a tentative appointment	CTRL+SHIFT+T
Cut	CTRL+X
Delete an appointment	CTRL+D
Edit an appointment	CTRL+E
Exit Schedule+	ALT+F4
Find an appointment	CTRL+F
Go to a specific date	CTRL+G
Move	CTRL+M
Move an appointment	CTRL+O
Open Help (context-sensitive)	F1
Paste	CTRL+V

To	Press
Print	CTRL+P
Set or remove a reminder	CTRL+SHIFT+R
Switch to the Appointment book	ALT+A
Switch to the Planner	ALT+P
Switch to the Task list	ALT+T
Switch to Today	ALT+Y
Undo	CTRL+Z
View tasks by project	CTRL+SHIFT+V

Microsoft Schedule+ Access Keys

To	Press
Arrange icons	ALT, W, A
Auto-Pick the first available time	ALT, M, A
Cascade windows	ALT, W, C
Copy an appointment	ALT, E, O
Copy selection to the Clipboard	ALT, E, C
Create a new appointment	ALT, M, N
Create a new project	ALT, K, P
Create a new task	ALT, K, T
Create a recurring appointment	ALT, M, R
Create a recurring task	ALT, K, R
Create an archive	ALT, F, A
Cut selection to the Clipboard	ALT, E, T
Delete an appointment	ALT, E, D
Edit a recurring appointment	ALT, M, C
Edit a recurring task	ALT, K, C
Edit an appointment	ALT, E, E
Exit and sign out	ALT, F, T

To	Press
Exit without signing out	ALT, F, X
Export appointments	ALT, F, E
Find an appointment	ALT, E, F
Get information about Microsoft Schedule+	ALT, H, A
Go to a specific date	ALT, E, G
Import appointments	ALT, F, I
Mark an appointment as private	ALT, M, P
Mark an appointment as tentative	ALT, M, T
Move an appointment	ALT, E, V
Move local file	ALT, F, L
Open an archive	ALT, F, N
Open another person's appointment book	ALT, F, O
Open Help Contents	ALT, H, C
Open Help Index	ALT, H, I
Paste information from the Clipboard	ALT, E, P
Print schedule or tasks	ALT, F, P
Resend a meeting notice	ALT, M, S
Set a reminder	ALT, M, M
Set up the printer	ALT, F, R
Show only active tasks	ALT, K, A
Sort tasks by description	ALT, K, D
Sort tasks by due date	ALT, K, B
Sort tasks by priority	ALT, K, I
Start online Demos	ALT, H, D
Tile windows	ALT, W, T
Turn off reminders	ALT, F, M
Undo last action	ALT, E, U
View tasks by project	ALT, K, V
Work offline or online	ALT, F, W

Working Offline with Microsoft Mail

This appendix discusses using Mail offline on a computer that is normally on-line. If your primary computer is at home or in another office, away from your mail network, a product called Microsoft Mail Remote for Windows can help you link up to your network from another computer. Mail Remote provides you with easy dial-in access to the main postoffice and several options for transferring messages back and forth.

Lesson 6 shows you how to export and import files that contain folders with messages so that you can transport the messages on a floppy disk and work with them on another computer. In this appendix, you will learn about what you can do on your own computer when you are not connected to the network. You can work with all of your stored messages in Microsoft Mail for Windows even if the network server is not available, or if you disconnect your computer from the network and take it home or on a trip. When you use Mail on a computer that is temporarily disconnected from your Mail server, you are working *offline*.

You can perform most of the Microsoft Mail for Windows functions that you learned about in Part 1 and Part 2 of this book when you are offline, except that you cannot receive new messages, change your password, or access the global Address Book. Only your Personal Address Book is available when you work offline. Although you can compose and address messages, when you press the Send button, they are held in your Outbox and cannot be delivered while you are offline.

When working offline, you can	When working offline, you cannot
Attach files from your disk to messages	Change your password
Compose and address messages	Create shared folders
Create private folders	Receive new messages
Delete messages	Use the global address list
Embed objects in messages	
Import and export message files	
Move messages between folders	
Send, reply to, and forward messages (but they are stored in your Outbox until your computer is online)	
Sort messages	
Use your Personal Address Book	

Working with Your Message File

Before you can work offline, you must be sure that you can access your existing messages. All of your messages and folders are stored in a *message file* that resides either on your network Mail server or on your local hard disk. If it is stored on the network server, you need to move this message file from the server to your local hard disk before you can work offline. Your message file is an active file that is automatically updated whenever you create, receive, or send a message. When you export folders (as you did in Lesson 6), you are copying or moving part of your message file.

In the Windows for Workgroups version of Microsoft Mail, the message file always resides on your local hard disk, since there is no server involved in the peer-to-peer network.

Note   This section and its exercises are optional. Check with your system administrator before you attempt to move your message file to your local disk. Also, check your hard disk to make sure you have enough space. Depending on the number of messages you have stored, your message file might require 800K or more of your disk space.

Move your message file to your computer's hard disk

1   From the <u>M</u>ail menu, choose <u>O</u>ptions.

The Options dialog box opens.

— *Server button*

2   In the Options dialog box, choose the Server button.

The Server dialog box opens.

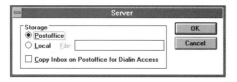

Note   The example shown here is taken from a Novell server-client network installation. Different brands and types of network setups might provide different options. Check with your system administrator for more details.

3   In the Storage area, select Local, if it is not already selected.

This indicates that your message file will be stored on your local drive. If Local is already selected, skip steps 4 and 5, and move to the next exercise.

4 In the File text box, type **c:\msmail\msmail.mmf** and then click OK.

This moves your message file to your C:\MSMAIL directory and names it MSMAIL.MMF.

5 In the Options dialog box, choose OK.

The Options dialog box closes and your message file is moved.

Once you have moved your message file, you can log off from your network and restart Microsoft Mail for Windows to work offline.

Restart Microsoft Mail for Windows offline

▶ Exit Microsoft Mail for Windows, log off from your network, and then restart Microsoft Mail for Windows offline.

Note The procedure for logging off from your network varies depending on your system setup. Follow your system's procedure for logging off from and logging on to the network in this appendix.

When you open Microsoft Mail offline, you see a symbol on the status bar with two network connections and a "no network" sign. This symbol reminds you that you are working offline.

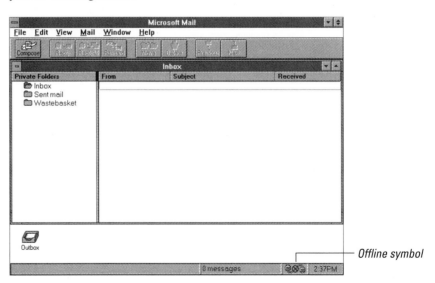

Offline symbol

Sending Messages Offline

When you create and send a new message while you're offline, the message waits in your Outbox until you are reconnected to the network server. When you are connected again, Mail automatically sends the message to the network postoffice and then on to the recipient's Inbox. The following illustration, representing a typical server-client network, shows what happens to your message when you send it while you are offline.

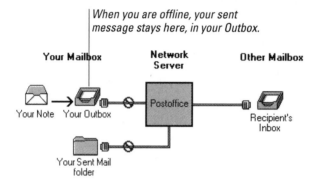

Notice that your message cannot move from your Outbox to the network server or to the recipient's Inbox while you are offline.

When someone else sends you a new message while you are offline, the message waits in the server until you are reconnected, and then it goes to your Inbox. You cannot receive new messages, even from yourself, until you are back online. The following illustration shows the path of a message sent to you from someone else while you are offline.

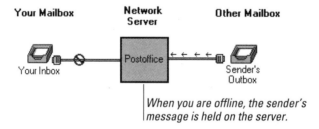

Note   If you like, have someone else on your network attempt to send a message to you while you are offline. When the person sends the message, it will go to the Mail server where it will wait until you are online again.

In the next exercise, you will send a message to yourself to see what happens when you send a message offline.

Compose and send a message offline

1   Double-click the Outbox icon.

Notice that the Outbox is currently empty. When you send a message in this exercise, the message will go to your Outbox and wait until you are back online to go to the addressee.

2   On the Outbox window, click the Minimize button.

3   Choose the Compose button.

The Send Note form opens.

4   In the To box, type your name, and then press TAB twice or click in the Subject box.

5   In the Subject box, type **Sending Offline** and then press TAB or click in the text area.

6   In the text area, type **What happens when a message is sent offline?**

7   Choose the Send button.

The message is sent. Because you are offline, you will not receive the message until you are back online.

8   Double-click the Outbox icon.

The Outbox opens. Notice that your Sending Offline message is now contained in the Outbox, waiting for the network connection to be restored.

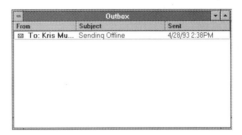

Receiving Messages When You Are Online Again

In order to receive your new incoming messages, you need to restart Microsoft Mail for Windows and attach to your Mail server again.

Restart Microsoft Mail for Windows online

▶ Exit Mail, exit Windows, log back on to your network and restart Microsoft Windows and Mail so that you can receive your new message.

A dialog box might open to inform you that your mailbox is being updated with the changes you made offline.

Now that you are online again, Microsoft Mail for Windows can deliver the message you sent to yourself. With the network connection restored, your message can now appear in your Inbox and a copy can be delivered to your Sent Mail folder. Messages that other people sent to you can also be delivered to your Inbox. In this exercise, you locate the message you sent and check your Sent Mail folder to see if a copy of the message is stored there.

Check for and delete your new message

1 From the View menu, choose New Messages.

A dialog box opens, informing you that Microsoft Mail is looking for your new messages.

2 Double-click your Inbox folder, if it is not open, to view the new message.

The "Sending Offline" message now appears in your Inbox.

3 Select the "Sending Offline" message, and then choose the Delete button.

4 Double-click your Sent Mail folder.

A copy of the "Sending Offline" message now appears in your Sent Mail folder.

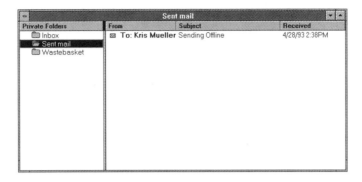

Note   It may take a few moments for a copy of your message to appear in the Sent Mail folder. If it does not appear, check your Mail Options to see if there is a check mark in the Save Copy Of Outgoing Messages In Sent Mail Folder option. If there is no check mark, this option is not selected and you will not receive a copy in your Sent Mail folder.

Move your message file back to the server

Note   Work through this exercise only if your message file was originally stored on the network Mail server. Check with your system administrator if you are not sure, or if you see different options than those shown here.

1   From the Mail menu, choose Options.

The Options dialog box opens.

Server button

2 In the Options dialog box, choose the Server button.

The Server dialog box opens.

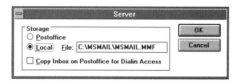

3 In the Storage area, select Postoffice.

This indicates that your message file will be stored on your network server.

4 In the Server dialog box, choose OK.

5 In the Options dialog box, choose OK.

The Options dialog box closes and your message file is moved back to the server.

Working Offline with Microsoft Schedule+

You can work with Microsoft Schedule+ even if the network Mail server is not available, or if you disconnect your computer from the network and take it home or on a trip. When you work with Microsoft Schedule+ on a computer that is temporarily disconnected from your network, you are working *offline*. Suppose that your system administrator needed to do some network maintenance and asked you to disconnect from the server. Or, perhaps you took your computer home for a day or two, but still needed to add appointments to your schedule or update your task list as you work. You can continue working on your schedule offline, without worrying about having to perform any complicated commands to update your online schedule when the connection is restored.

You can perform most of the Microsoft Schedule+ functions that you learned about in Part 3 of this book when you are offline, except that you cannot interact with other people on your network. Only your personal schedule is available offline.

When working offline, you can	When working offline, you cannot
Add daily notes	Request meetings
Add tasks to your schedule	View other people's schedules
Create and edit appointments	View responses to meeting requests
Create and edit tasks	
Move and delete appointments	
Set appointment reminders	
Set task priorities	
Set task reminders	
Sort tasks	

To work offline when Microsoft Schedule+ is already open, all you need to do is choose the Work Offline command from the File menu. This command disconnects you from your network connection for Microsoft Schedule+ and creates a local schedule file. If you are not already running Microsoft Schedule+ and you want to work offline, you must sign out of your mailbox before opening Microsoft Schedule+. After you are disconnected from your network connection, you can start Microsoft Schedule+ offline. You can work with your appointments and tasks offline, making any changes you need, and they will be stored in your local schedule file.

Working with Your Schedule File

Microsoft Schedule+ can have a schedule file both on the network server and on your local disk. When you make changes to your local schedule file offline and then restore your network connection, your network schedule file will be automatically updated with the changes. In the next exercise, you will start Microsoft Schedule+ and take it offline.

Start Microsoft Schedule+ and work offline

1   Double-click the Microsoft Schedule+ program icon to start Microsoft Schedule+, if it is not already running.

2   From the File menu, choose Work Offline.

If you have not worked offline with Microsoft Schedule+ before, you will not have a local file for your schedule. If this is the case, a dialog box will open, notifying you that a new file is being created. Notice that your Messages window is unavailable when you are working offline.

Now that Microsoft Schedule+ is offline, any changes that you make will be stored in the local schedule file. In the next exercise, you will create a practice appointment and task to demonstrate how your offline work is automatically updated when you restore your network connection.

Create a new appointment

1   Click the Today tab on your Schedule window.

The Appointment Book displays the current day's schedule.

2   Select a two-hour block of time, and then type **Offline Appointment**

Your new appointment is added to the Appointment Book.

3   Click the Tasks tab on the Schedule window.

The Task list opens.

4   In the New Task box, type **Offline Task** and then choose Add.

Your new task is added to the Task list.

5   Click the Planner tab on the Schedule window.

Notice that the Change Attendees button does not appear in the Schedule window. Since you are offline, you cannot interact with the other people on your network.

Restoring your network connection is as simple as removing it. All you need to do is choose the Work Online command, and your network connection is restored, with your new appointment and task added to your online schedule. In the next exercise, you will restore your network connection and check to be sure that your new appointment and task are in your online schedule.

Restore your network connection and update your schedule

1   From the File menu, choose Work Online.

A dialog box briefly appears as your schedule is updated with the changes you made offline. Notice that your Messages window is available again.

2   Choose the Today tab on the Schedule window.

Your "Offline Appointment" appears in your online schedule.

3   Select the appointment and then, from the Edit menu, choose Delete Appt.

4   Choose the Tasks tab on the Schedule window.

Your "Offline Task" appears in your Task list.

5   Select the task and choose the Delete button.

6   Choose the Planner tab on the Schedule window.

Notice that the Change Attendees button appears again in the Schedule window. Because you restored your network connection, you can once again coordinate with the other people on your network.

Importing and Exporting Schedule Files

In Lesson 6, you learned about importing and exporting folders in Microsoft Mail for Windows. Similarly, you can import and export schedule files in Microsoft Schedule+. To *export* your schedule, you choose the Export command from the File menu and select either your entire schedule or a specific date range. When you export, you automatically export both your appointments and your tasks. You can also choose to export your daily notes.

To *import* a schedule, you choose the Import command from the File menu and specify the name of the schedule file. Your schedule will be automatically updated with the appointment or task information from the imported file. If any appointments or tasks in the import file conflict with your existing appointments or tasks, a dialog box will open to inform you of the problem and allow you to resolve the conflict.

You can export your schedule file to other schedule program formats, or import files from other scheduling programs. To export to or import from another schedule program, you can use the Export or Import commands, and then select the correct file format.

Communicating with Other Mail Systems

Under certain circumstances, you can access other mail systems through Microsoft Mail for Windows. Your administrator might have set up one or more *gateways* that allow you to connect to other electronic mail systems. A gateway usually consists of software that acts as a message translator between Microsoft Mail for Windows and another mail system. Your network must be connected through a gateway in order for you to communicate with people on another system. Ask your Microsoft Mail system administrator if you need more information about the gateways currently installed on your network.

Note The ability to communicate with other mail systems is not available in the Windows for Workgroups version of Microsoft Mail. Ask your system administrator or workgroup administrator for more information about this option if communicating with other mail systems is a feature that you need.

When you send a message to a person on another mail system, it first travels through your network, and then through a gateway for translation to the other system. Then it goes through the other network and, finally, to the recipient's mailbox. The following illustration shows what typically happens to a message you send to someone on another mail system.

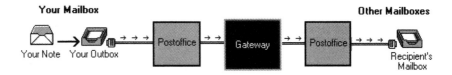

Active gateways are usually listed in your Address Book in the list of other available directories. The following steps illustrate the process you might go through to use a gateway to send a message.

To send a message to another mail system

1 Choose the Compose button on the tool bar.

2 Choose the Address button on the Send Note form.

   The Address Book opens.

Directories button

3 Click the Directories button.

4 From the list of gateways, select the name of the mail system you need, and then choose OK.

5 Select the name of the person you want to send your message to, and then click the To button.

Note If the name you need is not listed, you can add a name with the New Address button on the Address Book.

---

6 Choose OK.

7 Type your message subject and text, and then choose the Send button.

If you often send mail to people on other mail systems, you can add their names to your Personal Address Book, so that you don't need to go through the Address Book and the list of directories every time.

Note For more information about sending messages to people on other mail systems, see the topic "Sending Mail to Other Mail Systems" in Help. (This topic might not be available if you are running Microsoft Windows for Workgroups.)

The following table lists a representative sample of mail systems that you can communicate with and the gateways that you can use. For information about what gateways are available on your system, and how to address messages to other mail systems, check with your Mail administrator.

Mail system	Gateway(s)
ARCOM 400 Swiss PTT	X.400
AT&T Mail	X.400
Atlas 400	X.400
Atlas-Minitel	X.400
Banyan Mail	MHS or X.400
Beyond Mail	MHS
cc:Mail®	MHS, SNADS, or X.400
The Coordinator	MHS
CompuServe	SMTP or MHS
Data General® CEO	X.400
Da Vinci™	MHS
DEC All in 1	X.400, PROFS, or SNADS
DEC VMS®	X.400 or SNADS
Dutch PTT	X.400
Easylink®	X.400
Envoy 100/Gemdes	X.400
FAX	Fax
Fischer Int'l EMC2	X.400 or SNADS
Gold 400 UK	X.400
Higgins	MHS
IBM AS/400® Office	SNADS
IBM System 36	PROFS
IBM CMS NOTES	PROFS
IBM DISOSS	SNADS
IBM Office Vision™ MHS	SNADS
IBM PROFS®	PROFS
INFONET	X.400
Internet	SMTP
Lotus Notes®	MHS

Mail system	Gateway(s)
Microsoft Mail for AppleTalk	Microsoft Mail connection
Microsoft Mail to Microsoft Mail	Microsoft Mail connection
NCR–Cooperation	X.400
Novell MHS	MHS
Retix®	X.400
Softswitch Central	SNADS
Sprint Telectronic mail	X.400
Telebox 400 German PTT	X.400
Touch	X.400
Unisys	X.400
UNIX/SMTP	SMTP
UUCP	SMTP
Verimation Memo	SNADS
Wang® Office	MHS, X.400, or PROFS
X.25	X.400

Glossary

access privileges   The level at which other users can access your schedule in Microsoft Schedule+. Access privileges give others the ability to view, read, create, or modify your appointments and tasks in Microsoft Schedule+.

Address Book   A dialog box containing a list of all available addressees on your network, and any other gateways and networks, to whom you can send mail. You can use the Address Book to address your messages.

appointment   A block of time with a description on your Appointment Book in Microsoft Schedule+. Appointments can be private, tentative, overlapping, or recurring as well.

Appointment Book   A view in Microsoft Schedule+ that lets you see the description and times of your appointments for a day.

attaching   Sending a file with a message through Microsoft Mail for Windows. You can attach any type of file to a message.

Auto-Pick   A feature in Microsoft Schedule+ that automatically selects the first time available for a meeting on multiple people's schedules.

cascade   To arrange multiple windows in the application workspace so that you can view the contents of the active window and the title bars of the other windows.

chime   In Microsoft Mail for Windows, the sound that you hear when a new message arrives. You can turn the chime on or off in the Options dialog box.

Clipboard   An area in the computer's memory where information that has been cut or copied is stored until it is replaced by new information, or until you quit Windows.

composing   Creating a message in Microsoft Mail for Windows, including addressing the heading and entering and editing text.

Control menu   The menu on a window that allows you to move, size, minimize, maximize, and restore a window, close an application, switch to another window, or run another program.

default   In Microsoft Mail and Microsoft Schedule+, an option setting that is automatically chosen when you install the software. For example, in Microsoft Mail for Windows, one default is to save deleted messages in the Wastebasket until exiting. You can change default settings for either application in their respective Options dialog boxes.

embedding   Inserting an object into a message that you send through Microsoft Mail for Windows. Embedding, unlike attaching, does not use a separate file for the object; the object is part of the message.

exporting   In Microsoft Mail for Windows, saving a folder or folders to a separate file that can be imported on another computer, or saving a schedule in Microsoft Schedule+ to import on another computer. *See also* importing.

file   A unit of electronic information, such as a document or program, that has been named and stored on a disk.

folder   A container for organizing messages in Microsoft Mail for Windows. There are three standard folders: Inbox, Sent Mail, and Wastebasket. You can also create your own personal or shared folders.

forward   To send a received message to someone else by using the Forward button or command in Microsoft Mail for Windows. When you forward a message, a copy of the message is automatically appended to a new message that you can add text to and address.

gateway   Software that allows Microsoft Mail for Windows to communicate with other mail systems.

group name   An address that represents more than one person. For example, the group name "Accounting" can represent all of the people in the Accounting department. You can use a group name in the place of a single name in the To or Cc boxes in Microsoft Mail for Windows.

handle   In Microsoft Schedule+, an appointment handle appears at the top and bottom of a selected appointment. You can move the appointment with the top handle, or change its duration with the bottom handle.

importing   Bringing information from a message file into Microsoft Mail for Windows or from a schedule file into Microsoft Schedule+. *See also* exporting.

Inbox   The folder in Microsoft Mail for Windows that holds your new incoming messages.

insertion point   A blinking, vertical bar in the text area of the screen that indicates where characters you type will appear.

mailbox   Your storage area in Microsoft Mail for Windows' directory.

meeting request   A special message that originates and can be read in Microsoft Schedule+. Meeting requests have buttons that let you accept, decline, or tentatively accept an invitation to a meeting automatically, without creating a new message.

message   An electronic note that is sent through Microsoft Mail for Windows.

message file   A file that holds your messages and Personal Address Book. Your main message file resides either on the network server or on your hard disk.

MSMAIL.INI   A special program file that lets you set options for your Microsoft Mail for Windows interface.

note   In Microsoft Schedule+, a general comment that applies to the entire day, rather than a specific appointment, or a record of a completed task.

object   Any collection of information that can be stored in a file. You can embed objects from a file, such as an image, some text, or a table, into other files or documents.

offline   Disconnected from the network.

online   Connected to the network.

Outbox   A special window in Microsoft Mail for Windows that holds your outgoing messages until they are sent through the network. If you are working offline, messages you send remain in the Outbox until you are online.

overlapping appointment   An appointment whose time overlaps another appointment in Microsoft Schedule+.

password   A security feature of both Microsoft Mail for Windows and Microsoft Schedule+. Assigning a password to your mailbox or schedule ensures that other people cannot access your messages or appointments.

Personal Address Book   Your personal list of addressees, including any personal groups you have created. Your Personal Address Book is not accessible to other people on your network.

personal group   A group name that you create in Microsoft Mail for Windows. Personal groups are for your use only and are not available to others on your network.

Planner   A view in Microsoft Schedule+ that allows you to see which time slots are taken up by appointments for one to three weeks, depending on the size of your Schedule window.

pointer   The small, graphical object on your screen that is controlled by your mouse movements and that changes shape according to its location and function.

postoffice   A directory on the network that stores the program files and message files for Microsoft Mail for Windows.

priority   The level of importance or urgency of a message or a task. In Microsoft Mail for Windows, messages can have high, normal or low priorities. In Microsoft Schedule+, tasks can have any priority from 1–9 or A–Z.

private appointment   An appointment in Microsoft Schedule+ whose description does not appear on your schedule when another user opens it.

projects   Categories for tasks in Microsoft Schedule+.

recurring appointment   An appointment that occurs repeatedly on a regular basis. You can set the time period and frequency of a recurring appointment in Microsoft Schedule+.

recurring task   A task that occurs repeatedly. You can set the time period and frequency of a recurring task in Microsoft Schedule+.

reminder   A message that appears at a predetermined time before the scheduled start time of an appointment in Microsoft Schedule+. A bell symbol next to an appointment or task indicates that a reminder is set for that appointment or task.

reply   To compose a response to a message with the Reply button or command in Microsoft Mail for Windows. When you reply to a message, the recipient information is automatically filled in and the original message is appended to the response.

return receipt   An option that you can set for messages in Microsoft Mail for Windows. Return receipts notify you when your message has been received and read. The receipt includes sender, recipient, subject, date, and time information.

Sent Mail folder   A special folder that holds copies of messages that you send in Microsoft Mail for Windows. The option of automatically saving copies of your messages in the Sent Mail folder can be turned on or off.

server   A computer that stores and processes network files.

sorting   Arranging items in a particular order. In Microsoft Mail for Windows, you can arrange the display of your messages by Sender, Subject, Date, or Priority. In Microsoft Schedule+, you can arrange the display of your tasks by Project, Priority, Due Date, and Description.

subfolder   In Microsoft Mail for Windows, a folder within another folder.

task   In Schedule+, a particular assignment or duty that you need to accomplish. An item in a To Do list.

Task list   A view in Schedule+ that allows you to view and modify your tasks and projects.

template   A pre-addressed message, perhaps with the subject and some text already filled in, that you can store in your Inbox and use repeatedly.

tentative appointment   An appointment that is not firmly scheduled. If an appointment date or time is not certain, you can mark it as a tentative appointment in Microsoft Schedule+, and it will appear in your Appointment Book with a shaded background.

tile   In Microsoft Mail for Windows, to arrange multiple windows vertically in the application workspace so that you can view the contents of the windows.

Wastebasket   A special folder in Microsoft Mail for Windows that holds deleted messages. As an option, you can set the Wastebasket either to be emptied whenever you quit Microsoft Mail for Windows, or to hold messages until you actively delete them from the Wastebasket itself. (In the Windows for Workgroups version of Mail, the equivalent folder is named "Deleted Mail.")

Index

Note: Italicized page numbers refer to illustrations.

Catapult, Inc.

Catapult is a national software training company dedicated to providing the highest quality application software training. Years of PC and Macintosh instruction for major corporations and government institutions provide the models used in building Catapult's exclusive Performance-Based Training program. Based on the principles of adult learning, Performance-Based Training materials ensure that training participants leave the classroom with the ability to apply skills acquired during the training day.

Catapult's Product Development group is pleased to share their training skills with a wider audience through the Step by Step series. *Microsoft Mail for Windows* is the sixth in the Step by Step series to be produced by Catapult Press. This book and others in the series will help you develop the confidence necessary to achieve increased productivity with your Microsoft products.

Catapult's corporate headquarters are in Bellevue, Washington.

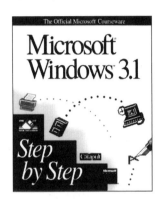
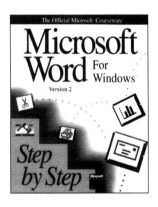
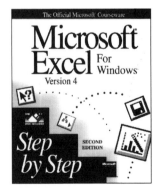
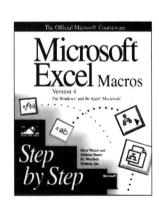